Nourish
SOUPS

Nourish
SOUPS

HEARTY SOUPS WITH
A HEALTHY TWIST

REBECCA WOODS

PHOTOGRAPHY BY LUKE ALBERT

quadrille

CONTENTS

Introduction

"Who doesn't love soup?" was the response most often received from friends and family when I told them the subject of this book. It turns out that everyone is surprisingly effusive on the matter of soup. The rows and rows of pots and cans of ready-made soup in supermarket aisles and chillers are testament to its belovedness. In fact, I suspect we're suspicious of anyone who claims not to eat soup at least once in a while.

Perhaps this is because it's tricky to dislike something that can literally be anything you want it to be. And to get all etymological on you, that's the whole point – 'soup', in its original sense, is a jumble, a mixture of different elements. You can add anything you like, to make it fit for any occasion – a light brothy starter in an Asian style on a summery day, or a hearty warming wintery mix, packed with satisfying grains and tender meat. But whatever you choose, it's never better than when you make it yourself... and there are few foods that won't taste good when suspended in a bowl of delicious broth.

But it goes beyond flavour, too; for me, soup is a food that is so inextricably intertwined with growing up – from a bowl of chicken soup on a sick day or a can of cream of tomato (there's a reason Warhol immortalized this) with a cheese toastie as a child, to a pot of noodly pho enjoyed on a plastic stool at the side of a Hanoi street, those happy memories bring comfort. It has unequalled nostalgic power that will ground you, not just physically, but emotionally, too.

I've tried to rein in my classic French cookery training and bring a healthy slant to the recipes here. They are wholesome, packed with fresh vegetables, whole grains and, for the most part, lean proteins. While a few liberties have been taken with a smidgen of butter, a drizzle of cream or a splash of alcohol here and there for that all-important flavour, on the whole I have kept them as concoctions that will leave you feeling nourished and energized, satisfied not soporific.

"Are there even 60 soup recipes?" one friend asked. Well, that's rather the point. There are as many as you want there to be. Let this book be just a starting point.

A few hints & tips

One of the joys of soup is its simplicity. There's very little that you need in the way of equipment or even cooking expertise. But there are a few hints and tips that might help you along the way, especially if you decide to go off-piste and devise your own soup concoctions rather than strictly following the recipes here – something I wholeheartedly encourage.

QUALITY INGREDIENTS

The simplicity of many of the soups here means that often they are only as good as their ingredients, especially when it comes to meat and fish. Try to buy the best produce that you can afford and your soup will be all the better for it. You can, of course, be a little more flexible with veggies – puréed soups are one of the best ways to be economical and use up vegetables that are a little past their best.

BROTHY OR CREAMY?

While a thick puréed and spiced root veg soup might be an ideal warmer-upper for a cold day, a light vegetable or seafood broth makes a great summer starter. There's no need to pick a favourite, but it's worth investing in a proper blender/liquidizer if you are going to be making lots of puréed soups – for speed and smoothness. Stick immersion blenders are great for partially blending soups to thicken them (see 'Thickening' opposite), but there will probably always be lumps that make it through if you're trying to blend the whole pan. Of course, many of the soups here have been left as broths, especially those including meat, which is less suitable for blending, and are better as hearty stewy soups.

COOKING TIMES

I've tried to include a mixture of methods, some very quick and simple, and others which depend on a more lengthy cooking process. While some of the cooking processes may seem a bit drawn out, sometimes there's no shortcut to deep flavour and tender meat (or beans in the case of the Slow-Baked Greek Bean Soup with Halloumi Croutons on page 90). Once a slow-cooked soup is bubbling away, it doesn't really need a lot of attention, so don't see it as extra work. It will also fill the house with deliciously comforting smells.

ADDING FLAVOUR

Keeping a basic storecupboard of liquid seasonings – such as soy sauce, Worcestershire sauce, balsamic vinegar, Tabasco, etc. – and dried herbs and spices means you will have plenty of tools to add a hit of flavour, should your soup need perking up a little. If you can find space in the garden or on the windowsill for a few pots of fresh herbs, too, their power can't be overstated.

A WORD ON SEASONING

For most healthy adults, seasoning food properly is not a health hazard. At the risk of antagonizing cardiologists everywhere, I'm inclined to believe that if you're enjoying freshly cooked homemade food at each meal of the day and keeping processed meals and snacks to an absolute minimum, it's very unlikely that you will be consuming too much salt by adding it to your soups, and the flavour will suffer if you don't use it. Season sagely...

THICKENING

If you're making a soup in which the main ingredient is a vegetable, especially a green, leafy one with a high water content, you'll need something to thicken it so that it feels more substantial. Potato is classically used for this, but I'm also a big fan of using rice, which adds a different, delicate flavour to the soup. You can also use cornflour [cornstarch], slaked with a drop of water then added back into the soup and cooked for a few minutes, like I have in the Malay Squash Chowder with Coconut & Lemon Grass on page 134. Or, you can simply blend a little of the soup (with a stick blender or by blitzing a little in a blender and returning it to the pan) and the small proportion of puréed solids will add body.

STOCK

I'm not a huge fan of dehydrated stock cubes. Sometimes, there's just no hiding that artificial tang they seem to imbue everything with, especially in more delicately flavoured soups, such as asparagus. Although, if you are adding lots of spices or starchy vegetables to a soup, they are usually fine, and are admittedly a lot cheaper than other options. I have provided the following recipes for basic stocks for meat, fish and vegetables, but if time is short, I know corners do need to be cut. Do try to use either a pot or pouch of ready-made stock, or at least the jelly stock pots, which don't seem to be so processed in flavour than the dried cubes. Several of the recipes have a stock written into the recipe, which it is best to follow for the optimum flavour – and to properly (slow) cook any meat or fish in the soup.

MEAT STOCK

MAKES ABOUT 1.5 LITRES [1½ QUARTS]

1.5kg [3¼lb] chicken or beef bones or carcasses (depending on the recipe) • a little olive oil, to drizzle • 2 large carrots, peeled and chopped into chunks • 1 large onion, halved • 2 celery sticks, chopped into chunks • 1 large leek, chopped into chunks • a bouquet garni made up of parsley stalks, thyme sprigs and a bay leaf • a few black peppercorns

---

Preheat the oven to 190°C fan (375°F) Gas 5.

Put the bones into a large roasting pan and drizzle with a little oil – not too much or you will have a fatty stock. Toss the bones to coat them in the oil, then roast for about 30 minutes until the bones are browned. You can skip this step and put the bones straight in the saucepan with the water, if you wish, but roasting the bones really does help bring out their meaty flavour.

Put the bones in a large saucepan, leaving any fat in the roasting pan, and add all the remaining ingredients. Cover with about 2.5 litres [11 cups] cold water, set the pan over a medium heat, cover loosely with a lid and bring the stock up to a simmer.

Once the stock is almost boiling, skim any scum from the surface with a large spoon. (Keep the spoon and a bowl at the side of the pan so you can skim it occasionally during cooking.) Reduce the heat to low and cook for about 2 hours, loosely covered, until well flavoured.

Strain the stock through a fine strainer to remove the bones and aromatics. Now you can transfer it to a clean saucepan and continue to cook it down to intensify the flavour, or simply put it in the fridge or freezer until needed.

FISH STOCK
MAKES ABOUT 1 LITRE [1 QUART]

1 Tbsp butter • 1 onion, diced • 1 fennel bulb, sliced • 150ml [⅔ cup] white wine • 1.25kg [2¾lb] white fish heads and bones or prawn [shrimp] shells, washed of any blood (don't use oily fish for stock) • a bouquet garni made up of parsley stalks, thyme sprigs and a bay leaf

———

Melt the butter in a large saucepan and gently sauté the onion and fennel for 5 minutes or so until well softened and translucent. Add the white wine and fish bones and cover with about 1.5–2 litres [6–8½ cups] cold water – enough to just cover the bones.

Set the pan over medium heat, cover loosely with a lid, and bring the water slowly up to a simmer. Once it is just about at boiling point, reduce the heat to low and leave to simmer gently for 20 minutes.

Strain the stock through a fine strainer to remove the fish bones and aromatics. Now you can transfer it to a clean saucepan and continue to cook it down to intensify the flavour, or simply put it in the fridge or freezer until needed.

VEGETABLE STOCK
MAKES ABOUT 1.5 LITRES [1½ QUARTS]

2 large onions, peeled and roughly diced • 3 large carrots, thickly sliced • 2 large leeks, thickly sliced • 2 celery sticks, thickly sliced • 2 whole garlic cloves, peeled • 1 large fennel bulb, roughly chopped • a bouquet garni made up of parsley stalks, thyme sprigs and a bay leaf • a few black peppercorns

———

Put everything into a large saucepan and cover with about 1.5 litres [6½ cups] water. Set the pan over medium heat, cover loosely with a lid, and bring the water slowly up to the boil. Once it is just about at boiling point, reduce the heat to low and leave to simmer gently for 30 minutes.

Strain the stock through a fine strainer to remove the vegetables and aromatics, then store in a container in the fridge or freezer until required.

Soup toppers

Finishing off a bowl of soup with a sprinkle of something not only makes it more appealing to the eye and adds extra flavour, but also adds textural contrast – useful if you've made a more homogeneous blended soup. There are endless possibilities to add that bit of complementary flavour and texture.

CLASSIC CROUTONS

SERVES 4–6

3 thick slices of sourdough bread, cut into cubes • 2–3 Tbsp olive oil • sea salt flakes

---

Preheat the oven to 190°C fan (375°F) Gas 5. Put the bread in a large bowl and drizzle over the olive oil. Season well with the sea salt flakes and toss everything together so that the bread is well coated in the oil. Spread the cubes out on a baking sheet and bake for 10–12 minutes, stirring halfway through, or until turning golden and crispy.

CHEESY POLENTA CROUTONS

SERVES 4–6

100g [⅔ cup] fine polenta [cornmeal] • 1 tsp sea salt flakes (use less if using fine salt) • 50g [¾ cup] finely grated Parmesan • 25g [2 Tbsp] butter

---

Put the polenta in a saucepan with 400ml [1¾ cups] water and heat over a low–medium heat, stirring all the time, until it comes to the boil. Once boiling, cook, still stirring constantly, for about 6–7 minutes until smooth and no longer grainy. Stir in the salt, Parmesan and butter and cook for another couple of minutes until the butter and cheese have melted. Tip the polenta onto a non-stick baking sheet and form into a square roughly measuring 18 x 18cm [7 x 7in] and about 1.5cm [⅝ in] thick. Leave to cool and set.

To finish the croutons, turn out the block of polenta and cut it into 1.5cm [⅝ in] dice. Heat a non-stick (this is essential – don't try this in anything without a non-stick coating) frying pan over a medium–high heat and fry the polenta cubes, a few at a time, until they are golden brown on all sides.

NUTS & SEEDS

Nuts and seeds, especially toasted ones, are a great healthy way to add a bit of extra flavour and texture to soups and boost their nutritional value, too. Hazelnuts, almonds, cashews, walnuts, pine nuts and pumpkin, hemp and watermelon seeds have all been suggested throughout the book, but don't feel limited to these. Experiment and sub in whatever you think may work – or whatever opened packs you have lurking at the back of the cupboard...

DRIZZLES

Herb-based sauces such as pesto, chimichurri and salsa verde make a great last-minute addition, drizzled over the final soup. Adding herbs like this, post cooking, keeps their fresh punchy flavour, which can lift a soup.

Likewise, using strongly flavoured oils such as toasted sesame, walnut or hazelnut oils; extra virgin olive oil; or oils that have been flavoured with chilli or lemon, for example, can add depth and richness to the soup. And never underestimate the power of a good squeeze of lime or lemon juice to lift flavour.

SHOPPABLE TOPPERS

A stroll around the supermarket aisles reveals plenty of other choices for things that can add interest to a humble soup.

Shop the chilled aisle for crème fraîche, soured cream or Greek yogurt to cool down spicy soups, or cheeses such as Stilton, Parmesan or goat's cheese to add a sharpness to richer ones.

Shards of crisp golden bacon, tiny scallops or ribbons of smoked salmon help an everyday bowl of soup feel a bit more of an occasion and add a protein boost that can turn it from a light lunch into a satisfying meal.

Crispy fried onions or salted popcorn add a pleasing crunch, or you could even try a handful of granola over smooth wintery soups, such as pumpkin or mushroom. Shop with an open mind!

Finally, fresh ingredients such as herbs, rocket [arugula], sliced radishes (pickled or not – see page 24), or just some lemon or lime zest finely grated over the top can all help you to easily customize your soup to reflect how you feel that day.

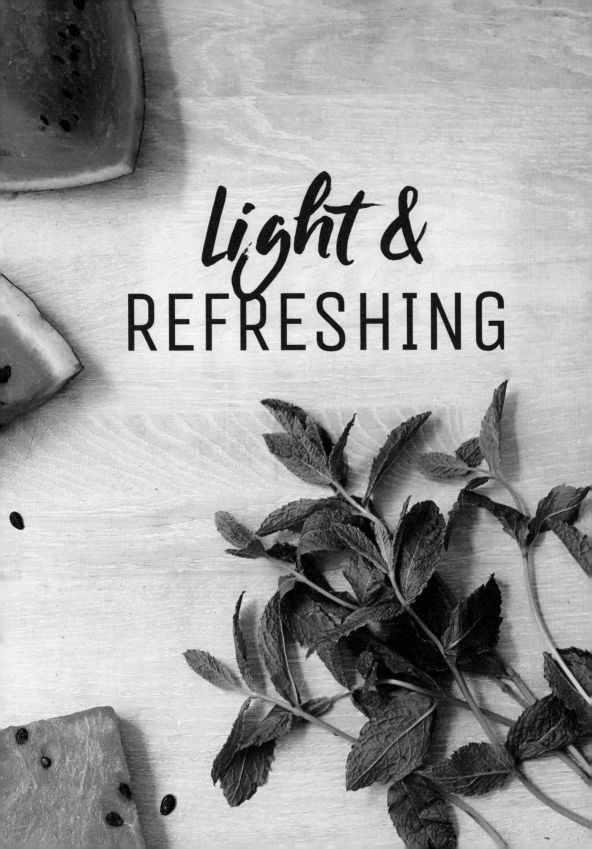

Light &
REFRESHING

Jerk Chicken

WITH CHARRED CORN, PEPPERS & PINEAPPLE

The surprise star here turned out to be the lowly, unsuspecting and fast-ripening slice of fresh pineapple lurking at the back of the fridge. I had originally thought that the injection of lovely acidic fruitiness needed to balance the soup should be provided by a good squeeze of lime juice, but how wrong I was.

Slice the chicken into thin strips and put it in a bowl with the jerk seasoning, 2 tsp of the oil, the thyme and a good pinch of salt. Leave to marinate for a couple of hours in the fridge, or overnight if possible.

Heat the remaining 1 tsp oil in a large non-stick saucepan and fry the chicken over high heat until it is browned and caramelizing on the outside. Turn the heat down to medium, add the spring onion whites and Scotch bonnets and cook for a few minutes until everything is softened. Add the stock and let it bubble away for a few more minutes until the chicken is cooked through.

Meanwhile, heat a grill [broiler] to its highest setting. Drizzle the corn cob with a little oil and grill, turning frequently, until it is catching and charred all over (not completely black – you still want some yellow). You could also do this more quickly with a chef's blowtorch, if you have one. Allow the cob to cool a little until you can handle it, then slice the kernels off the cob with a sharp knife.

Add the corn to the soup, along with the peppers and kidney beans, and cook for 2–3 minutes, until the peppers are just softening, but you still have a fresh crunch, and the beans are heated through. Add the pineapple and spring onion greens, season well with salt and pepper and cook for a few more seconds, just until they are heated through.

Ladle into bowls and sprinkle with a little more thyme to serve.

SERVES 4 | DAIRY-FREE

4 skinless, boneless chicken
    thighs
1½ Tbsp jerk seasoning
1 Tbsp groundnut oil,
    plus extra to drizzle
leaves from a few sprigs
    of soft summer thyme,
    plus extra to serve
10 spring onions [scallions],
    finely sliced and white and
    green parts separated
2 Scotch bonnet chillies,
    finely sliced (discard the
    seeds to keep the heat
    down, if wished)
1.2 litres [5 cups] good chicken
    stock
1 corn on the cob
½ green [bell] pepper, diced
½ red [bell] pepper, diced
1 x 400g [14oz] can red kidney
    beans, drained and rinsed
125g [4½oz] diced fresh
    pineapple
sea salt and freshly ground
    black pepper

Prawn & Pernod Broth

WITH PINK PEPPERCORNS & ASIAN GREENS

A love of alliteration is not the only reason I put these ingredients together... This one's a light starter on a balmy summer's eve when you're in the relaxed, chilled-glass-of-Sauvignon-at-arm's-reach-induced mindset to appreciate the subtle interplay between the shellfish and anise flavours, plus a little spicy hit when you bite on an aromatic pink peppercorn. If you make the Chunky Creole Fish Stew with Pepper & Tomato on page 72, keep the prawn heads and shells and use them to intensify this stock – you can just pop them in the freezer until needed.

To make the stock, peel the prawns and put the heads and shells in a large saucepan. Add all the remaining ingredients and cover with 1.4 litres [6 cups] water. Cover and bring to a simmer over medium heat, skimming off any foam or scum from the top as it accumulates. As soon as the liquid is simmering, remove the lid and lower the heat to medium–low. Allow to simmer gently, uncovered, for about 30 minutes. Allow the stock to cool a little, then strain and return to a clean saucepan.

Add the spring onion whites, fennel and pink peppercorns to the stock and simmer for 4–5 minutes, until the fennel is tender. Taste and season the stock well with salt – it will take quite a lot – but you shouldn't need any more pepper.

Add the prawns to the stock along with the spring onion greens and the Pernod and cook for 3 minutes more, or until the prawns are just cooked and their flesh is opaque.

Sprinkle a few Japanese leaves into the bottom of 4 shallow bowls. Ladle the broth between the bowls, dividing the prawns evenly between the bowls, then serve.

SERVES 4 | DAIRY-FREE

For the stock:
heads and shells from the prawns [shrimp] – see below, plus prawn heads and shells you've collected and frozen (or ask your fishmonger)
1 onion, peeled and quartered
1 large leek, chopped into chunks
1 large carrot, chopped into chunks
1 celery stick, chopped into chunks
a few black peppercorns

For the broth:
6 spring onions [scallions], finely sliced on a deep angle, white and green parts separated
2 bulbs baby fennel, shredded very finely on a mandoline
2 tsp pink peppercorns
400g [14oz] large fresh prawns [shrimp] in their shells
2 Tbsp Pernod
a large handful of Japanese greens (such as baby leaf Japanese spinach and baby purple pak choi/bok choy)
sea salt

Raw Sorrel & Avocado
WITH WHIPPED LEMON RICOTTA

Having just decamped from London and traded a first-floor apartment with no outside space, for a place with a garden, the first thing I have done is plant several sorrel plants. Unjustly hard to find in supermarkets (although if you have a decent local farmers market, you'll probably be lucky), sorrel is probably the most wonderful foodstuff that people don't know about. Cooking this tangy and citrusy herb impairs it, in my opinion. Keep it raw and it will not only keep its vibrant colour, but also its wonderfully sharp citrusy bite, which has been balanced here with the addition of creamy avocado and a serving of velvety whipped ricotta, scented with lemon zest. While we all know there are a lot of raw green soups that taste just that bit too, well, 'green', I'm happy to say this isn't one of them.

Put the ricotta in a mixing bowl with the lemon zest and beat it with an electric hand whisk until well combined. Season with a little salt and pepper and set aside.

Put all the soup ingredients in a high-speed blender and blitz until smooth. Season with salt and pepper.

Pour the soup into small bowls or wide cups (you only need small servings of this), top with a spoonful of the lemon ricotta and serve immediately.

SERVES 4 | VEGETARIAN

100g [3½oz] sorrel leaves
200g [7oz] peeled and roughly diced avocado flesh (about 1 smallish avocado)
250g [9oz] cucumber, roughly chopped into chunks
450ml [2 cups] coconut water, ice cold

For the whipped lemon ricotta:
150g [5½oz] ricotta cheese (opt for a vegetarian alternative if necessary)
finely grated zest of 1 small lemon
sea salt and freshly ground black pepper

Sweet & Smoky Tomato

WITH CHORIZO & SQUID

There are two ways to cook squid – quick and blisteringly hot or more gentle and drawn-out. I tried this both ways and opted for the latter, perhaps because, like the Slow-Cooked Lamb with Tomato, Fennel Seed & Farro soup (page 77), it began life as a favourite sauce for pasta, and ragùs seem to call for slow cooking. But it's no more work – once it's bubbling happily, you can walk away and let it do its thing, safe in the knowledge that the squid will be deliciously tender in the end. It still works well as a pasta sauce – just remove the lid and keep cooking to reduce the liquid right down, then stir in some cooked pasta and a handful or two of rocket right at the end.

Preheat the oven to 190°C fan (375°F) Gas 5.

Heat the oil in a large saucepan set over high heat and add the chorizo. Cook until it is browned and beginning to release its oils. Reduce the heat to low–medium and add the onion, garlic and a good pinch of salt. Cook for about 6 minutes until the onions are really beginning to soften. Add the smoked paprika and cook for a couple more minutes, then add the stock, passata, tomatoes, thyme and the squid. Put a lid on the pan and leave to bubble gently for about 1¼ hours, or until the squid is really tender.

Meanwhile, put the peppers on a baking sheet and drizzle with a little olive oil. Roast in the preheated oven for 25–30 minutes until they are soft and the skins are beginning to char. Remove them from the sheet with tongs, put them immediately into a bowl and cover with cling film [plastic wrap] or a plate. Leave them for 15 minutes or so – the trapped steam will help the skins come off. Once cool enough to handle, peel off and discard the skins and thinly slice the peppers.

Once the soup has had its time, tip in the peppers, along with any juices that may have collected in the bottom of the bowl. Season well with salt and pepper and serve in warmed bowls with a small handful of rocket on the top of each.

SERVES 4

2 Tbsp olive oil, plus a drizzle for the peppers
160g [5½oz] chorizo, diced
1 large onion, finely diced
3 garlic cloves, finely chopped
1 Tbsp sweet smoked paprika (pimentón dulce)
600ml [2½ cups] light fish stock (just use 1 jelly fish stock pot with 600ml hot water)
500ml [generous 2 cups] passata [strained tomatoes]
1 x 400g [14oz] can chopped tomatoes
leaves from 2 bushy thyme sprigs
1 squid tube, cleaned and thinly sliced into rings (include the tentacles, too, sliced up)
2 large red [bell] peppers, halved and deseeded
sea salt and freshly ground black pepper
rocket [arugula], to serve

Fresh Asparagus

WITH SWEET PICKLED RADISH & HEMP SEED

Asparagus' delicate flavour can be easily overpowered by a strong stock; you can sub out the homemade stock for a shop-bought one if you must, but there does carry with this the risk of the artificial tang of processed bouillon bullying its way through the subtle asparagus. The only – gentle – sharpness here should be from the contrasting colourful sweet radish pickles, while the hemp seeds add a rich, nutty flavour.

Heat the oil in a large saucepan and add the onion, leek, carrots, fennel and celery. Sauté over medium heat for 10 minutes or so until the vegetables are starting to pick up some colour.

Add 1.2 litres [5 cups] of water, the mushrooms, bay leaf, parsley stalks, peppercorns and garlic. Bring to a simmer (not a rolling boil) and leave to bubble away gently for about 30 minutes.

To prepare the radishes, put the sliced radishes in a shallow bowl. In a small jug or bowl combine the vinegar and honey and stir until the honey has completely dissolved. Pour this over the radishes and leave to pickle for about 30 minutes or so, stirring everything around occasionally, while you make the soup. I think they are nicer still a little crisp, so don't leave them much longer than this or they'll go a bit too floppy. Drain the radishes well and set aside.

Once the 30 minutes is up, strain the stock into a clean saucepan. As you are blending the soup and so don't need to worry about the stock being cloudy, you can use a spoon to push the stock through the sieve, mashing the vegetables a little to get out all the liquid and flavour. Add the potato to the stock and bring it to a simmer over a medium heat. Cover the pan and cook for about 12 minutes, or until the potato is almost cooked. Add the asparagus, cover again, and cook for a further 4–5 minutes, or until the asparagus is just tender.

Transfer the soup to a liquidizer and blend until smooth. Add the crème fraîche and blitz again until well incorporated. Taste and season with salt and black pepper.

Ladle the soup into bowls and top each bowl with a teaspoon of crème fraîche, some little radish stepping stones (you can serve the rest on the side) and a sprinkling of shelled hemp seeds.

SERVES 4 | VEGETARIAN

2 Tbsp olive oil
1 onion, diced
1 leek, sliced
2 carrots, peeled and sliced
1 fennel bulb, diced
1 celery stick, sliced
100g [3½oz] button
    mushrooms
1 bay leaf
a bunch of parsley stalks
a few black peppercorns
2 garlic cloves, peeled and
    lightly bashed with the side
    of a knife
150g [5½oz] peeled and diced
    potato
500g [1lb 2oz] trimmed
    asparagus spears
4 Tbsp crème fraîche,
    plus 4 tsp to serve
sea salt and freshly ground
    black pepper
shelled hemp seeds, to serve

For the pickled radishes:
100g [3½oz] radishes, very
    thinly sliced
3 Tbsp white rice vinegar
2 Tbsp clear honey

Salmon & Miso Broth

WITH UDON, EDAMAME & SHIITAKE

All of the usual indicators of fullness seem to abandon me when I make this. I guess it's the miso that should be thanked – that moreish, umami master encouraging furtive slurps directly from the ladle each time the pan is casually, yet repeatedly, passed. For that very reason, miso is not something to be compromised on here; if the supermarket doesn't have the sweet white variety, go to a health food store. It will make all the difference to the flavour.

Heat the oil in a large pan over a low heat and fry the ginger and garlic gently for 3-4 minutes until smelling fragrant. Add the mushrooms and cook for another minute or so until just wilted.

Add the stock to the pan, then stir in the mirin. Add the noodles, turn up the heat to medium–high and bring to the boil. Add the edamame, and bring back to the boil. Once boiling again, add the white parts of the pak choi and spring onions and return the heat to boiling. Cook for a few minutes until the liquid is hot and bubbling again.

Add the miso and stir in, then check the noodles – they should be very close to being perfectly cooked before you add anything else. Add the salmon pieces and pak choi greens and cook for 1–2 minutes maximum, until the salmon is just cooked and the greens are wilted. Season with salt, if needed.

Spoon the broth between 4 warmed bowls and sprinkle with the spring onion greens to serve.

SERVES 4

2 Tbsp vegetable oil

5cm [2in] piece fresh ginger, peeled and grated

2 garlic cloves, crushed

120g [4oz] shiitake mushrooms, sliced

1.2 litres [5 cups] hot good-quality fish stock (use prepared stock or jelly stock pots if not making your own, not cubes)

1 Tbsp mirin

100g [3½oz] dried brown rice udon noodles

150g [5½oz] frozen shelled edamame beans

2 heads of pak choi [bok choy], sliced and white and green parts separated

6 spring onions [scallions], sliced and white and green parts separated

4 Tbsp sweet white miso paste

350g [12oz] salmon fillet, skinned and cut into 2cm [¾in] dice

sea salt (optional)

Cidery Ham Hock

WITH SPRING GREENS & PEAS

We know how much pork and apple love a liaison, so it wasn't too far a stretch to switch a bit of the stock for some cider. The cider adds a slight sweetness to the already salty ham – a crack combination, if ever there was one – which makes this pretty irresistible. If by some miracle a portion or two does make it through to the next day, it will probably have set solid because of the gelatine in the stock. Just reheat it, adding a splash of water if needs be, and it will be as good as new, if not improved by the flavours having had a night to get better acquainted.

Soak the ham hock for 6–8 hours, changing the water every couple of hours to get rid of any excess salt.

Stick the cloves into the onion and put them in a large pan with the remaining stock ingredients. Add the ham hock and just cover with water (no more than 2 litres/8½ cups). Pop a lid on and bring to the boil over a medium heat. Skim the surface of the stock, then turn the heat down to low–medium and leave to simmer for 2 hours. Remove the lid towards the end of cooking to start the stock reducing, but make sure the meat is still submerged in liquid so it doesn't dry out.

Strain the stock, discarding the veg and reserving the ham. Transfer the stock to a clean pan and cook down until you have reduced it to 1.2 litres [5 cups] stock.

Meanwhile, and once the ham is cool enough to handle, shred the meat from the bone, cover and set aside.

Heat the oil and butter in a large saucepan and add the onion, celery and garlic. Cook over a low heat for about 10 minutes until well softened. Add the cider and turn up the heat. Cook for about 10 more minutes, or until the cider has reduced by about half.

Add the reduced stock and bring back to the boil, then add the peas, spring greens and the shredded meat. Cook for just a minute or so to warm the meat through and cook the veggies. Taste and season with salt, if needed, and plenty of black pepper.

Stir in the herbs just before serving, ladle into bowls and serve, with mustard on the side, if wished.

SERVES 4–6

For the ham and stock:
1.2kg [2½lb] smoked ham hock
1 large onion, halved
2 large carrots, roughly chopped
4 whole cloves
1 large leek, chopped into chunks
2 celery sticks, chopped
a few black peppercorns
a bouquet garni made from a few parsley stalks (save the leaves for the soup), a bay leaf and a sprig of thyme

For the soup:
1 Tbsp light olive oil
1 Tbsp butter
1 onion, finely diced
1 celery stick, finely sliced
1 garlic clove, crushed
500ml [2 cups] artisan [hard] cider
200g [1½ cups] frozen peas, thawed
150g [3 cups] shredded spring greens (remove any tough looking stalks or mangy outside leaves)
a small handful of mint leaves, roughly chopped
a small handful of flat-leaf parsley, roughly chopped
sea salt and freshly ground black pepper
English mustard, to serve (optional)

Sweet & Sour Med Veg
WITH OLIVE OIL CROUTES

Pomegranate molasses is a much neglected ingredient. Its beautiful Middle-Eastern patterned packaging is so alluring on the supermarket shelf... but you get it home and that promising bottle soon gets pushed to the back of the cupboard, not to see the cold light of day for months, if not years. But any lack of imagination should reflect badly on us, not the molasses, as it can add depth and a wonderful sweet and sour element to a pan of almost anything.

Preheat the oven to 180°C fan (350°F) Gas 4.

Tip the aubergine, courgette, onion and peppers onto a large baking sheet. Add the garlic cloves, sprinkle over the thyme leaves and drizzle over all the olive oil. Mix everything together well so that all the veg is coated in the oil. Roast for 30 minutes, stirring halfway through, until everything is soft and golden.

Meanwhile, cut a cross in the base of each tomato and put them in a heatproof bowl. Pour over boiling water to cover and leave them for about 20 seconds. Fish the tomatoes out with a slotted spoon and peel the skin off, then deseed and dice them.

Put the stock into a large saucepan with the tomatoes and bring up to a simmer.

Once the vegetables are roasted, pick the onions off the baking sheet and discard any dried, papery skin. Chop them down into rough dice. Squeeze the garlic cloves out of their skins and roughly chop those too – they should be breaking down almost to a paste. Tip them into the soup along with all the other veg and leave to simmer for about 10 minutes: the tomatoes and aubergine will start to break down and thicken the soup.

Meanwhile, for the croutes, heat a griddle pan until very hot. Drizzle the slices of bread with olive oil and press them onto the hot griddle. Toast for about 4 minutes on each side, or until black lines appear.

Add the pomegranate molasses to the soup and season with salt and pepper. Stir in the basil leaves just before serving. Ladle into 4 warmed bowls, scatter over a few extra basil leaves and drizzle with extra virgin olive oil. Serve with the croutes, fresh from the griddle, on the side.

SERVES 4 | VEGAN

1 large aubergine [eggplant] (or 2 small), diced
1 courgette [zucchini], diced (slightly smaller than the aubergine)
1 red onion, cut into 6 wedges lengthways
2 red [bell] peppers, chopped into chunks
4 large garlic cloves, unpeeled
leaves from a few thyme sprigs
4 Tbsp olive oil
4 large tomatoes (about 450g/1lb)
1 litre [4¼ cups] vegetable stock
2 Tbsp pomegranate molasses
a large handful of basil leaves, roughly ripped up, plus extra small leaves to serve
sea salt and freshly ground black pepper

For the croutes:
thick slices of crusty bread
extra virgin olive oil, to drizzle, plus extra to serve

Coconut & Coriander Fish

WITH KAFFIR LIME & BABY VEG

For a quick, light lunch, this soup is hard to beat. Gently infused with Asian aromatics and sweet coconut, it somehow manages to work as a summer refresher or a winter warmer, and can be on the table in less than half an hour. If you want to bulk it out a bit, add some rice noodles towards the end of cooking.

Put the fish stock in a saucepan and add the lime leaves, ginger, garlic, spring onion whites, chilli and coriander stalks. Bring the liquid to a simmer, then simmer for 20 minutes, with the lid on, until the stock is well infused with the flavours.

Strain the stock into a clean pan and add the coconut milk. Bring the liquid up to a simmer again (don't boil once the milk is added) and add the baby corn. Cook for about 3 minutes until it is beginning to soften. Add the mange tout and sea bass and cook for 2–3 minutes more, until the fish is just cooked and all the veg is tender but with a little crisp bite.

Stir in most of the coriander leaves and spring onion greens, then season with a good squeeze of lime juice and a little salt.

Ladle into 4 warmed bowls and serve topped with the reserved coriander and spring onion greens, and with lime wedges on the side for squeezing over.

SERVES 4 | DAIRY-FREE

800ml [3⅓ cups] fish stock, preferably homemade

10 fresh kaffir lime leaves

5 large slices fresh ginger

3 garlic cloves, whole but bashed

8 spring onions [scallions], greens sliced on the diagonal and whites halved lengthways

½ green chilli, halved lengthways

1 small bunch coriander [cilantro], stalks separated and leaves roughly chopped

1 x 400ml [14oz] can coconut milk

100g [3½oz] baby corn, halved lengthways

50g [2oz] mange tout [snow peas] or sugar snap peas, halved on the diagonal

2 sea bass fillets, chopped into chunks

a squeeze of lime juice

sea salt

lime wedges, to serve

Black Olive Borscht

WITH ORANGE & OREGANO

The inclusions (and omissions) suggested to the classic beetroot broth here take this soup from Kiev by way of Kefalonia. But they are an interesting twist and the lighter flavours present the challenge of getting the balance perfectly right – no single flavour should dominate. Master that and you will be rewarded.

Preheat the oven to 180°C fan (350°F) Gas 4.

Wrap the beetroots in kitchen foil together and place on a baking sheet. Bake for 1 hour, or until tender. Once cooked, rub the skins away – they should slip off easily – and grate the beetroots, discarding the stalks.

Heat the oil in a large saucepan set over low heat and add the onion, carrot, celery and garlic. Sauté very gently for about 15 minutes, or until everything is well softened and the onions are translucent.

Add the stock and bring to the boil, then lower the heat so the liquid is just simmering and add the orange juice and zest, oregano, olives and grated beetroot. Heat through for a few minutes until everything is warm, then season really well with salt and pepper.

Ladle into bowls and top with a sprinkle more oregano to serve, if you like.

SERVES 4 | DAIRY-FREE

500g [1lb 2oz] beetroot [beet] (try and get them all roughly the same size so they cook evenly – I used 5, about 100g [3½oz] each)
2 Tbsp olive oil
1 onion, finely diced
1 carrot, peeled and finely diced
1 celery stick, finely diced
1 large garlic clove, finely chopped
1.2 litres [5 cups] good beef stock, preferably homemade
juice of ½ orange (about 3 Tbsp), freshly squeezed
1 tsp finely grated orange zest
2 Tbsp finely chopped fresh oregano, plus optional extra to serve
30g [1oz] black olives, finely sliced
sea salt and freshly ground black pepper

Tofu & Carrot Broth
WITH SESAME

Like any good stock, this takes time to make, so it's worth doubling up and making a big batch of this broth, as it has a sort of restorative power, like a vegan bone broth. Its intense savouriness and depth of flavour comes from several umami-rich ingredients: dried seaweed, miso and shiitake mushrooms. If you have brown miso, that's fine and just add 1 tablespoon, but the broth colour, taking on the hue of the carrots and red pepper, remains more vibrant if you use white.

Preheat the oven to 190°C fan (375°F) Gas 5.

Put the pepper, carrots, leek, onion, celery and garlic cloves on a large baking sheet. Drizzle with a little oil and mix everything around so all the vegetables are lightly coated. Put in the oven and bake for about 40 minutes, stirring halfway through, until everything is wilted and caramelizing.

Tip everything from the baking sheet into a large saucepan and cover with 1.2 litres [5 cups] cold water. Add the kelp knots, dried shiitake, parsley stalks and peppercorns. Bring the liquid to the boil, then reduce the heat and simmer gently for 30 minutes. Strain and tip the stock into a clean pan. Stir in the miso and season well with salt. Keep warm over a low heat while you prep the serving ingredients.

Heat a large non-stick frying pan over medium heat and add the sesame seeds. Dry toast for 3 minutes or so, stirring, until they are turning golden and smelling toasty. Immediately tip them out onto a plate.

Add the oil to the same frying pan and fry the tofu for about 5 minutes, stirring frequently, until golden on all sides.

Ribbon the carrots on a vegetable peeler and divide between 4 warmed shallow bowls. Pour in the broth and the carrots will wilt and cook a little in the hot liquid. Divide the fried tofu evenly between the bowls. Finish each serving with a sprinkling of the toasted sesame seeds and a drizzle of toasted sesame oil.

SERVES 4 | VEGAN

For the broth:
1 red [bell] pepper, chopped
  into chunks
3 large carrots, sliced
1 large leek, sliced
1 large onion, roughly sliced
1 celery stick, sliced
3 garlic cloves, cut in half
a drizzle of light olive oil
5 kelp knots (or about 8g [¼oz]
  of other dried seaweed)
8g [¼oz] dried shiitake
  mushrooms
a bunch of parsley stalks
6 black peppercorns
2 Tbsp white miso paste
sea salt

To serve:
2 Tbsp sesame seeds
1 Tbsp olive oil
1 x 225g [8oz] pack firm
  smoked tofu, diced
6 long skinny carrots in a
  variety of colours
toasted sesame oil, to drizzle

Springtime Broth

WITH RHUBARB, & MINT & PISTACHIO PESTO

I'm forever being given bags of rhubarb by family who can't cope with a prolific crop. While vegetable patches are a ridiculously relaxing way to spend a Sunday afternoon pottering, when the same old vegetables appear at every meal, tedium is not far behind. Finding new ways to use the harvest is half the fun, and there are only so many buttery, sugary crumbles a person can eat before becoming the size of a house. Instead, try adding rhubarb to this healthful veggie broth for a wonderfully tangy base; it will break down and provide a fresh, fruity background flavour, so there's no need to worry about biting into sour chunks of it.

Put the butter in a large saucepan set over low heat and let it melt. Add the rhubarb and cook gently for about 5 minutes until it's starting to soften. Add the spring onion whites and cook for another minute, then add the stock and bring the liquid up to the boil.

Mix the cornflour with a little water in a small bowl. Add it to the pan and cook for a few minutes until the broth starts to thicken a little.

Meanwhile, put all the ingredients for the pesto in a mini chopper or the small bowl of a food processor and blitz until smooth. Season well with salt and pepper and set aside.

Add the sugar snaps, asparagus and broccoli to the broth and cook for 3 minutes, then add the broad beans, peas and spring onion greens and cook for 1 minute more. Stir in the herbs, then taste and season well with salt and pepper.

Serve the soup immediately (so the veg are still a little crisp and still bright green), in warmed shallow bowls with a dollop of pesto on top.

SERVES 4 | VEGETARIAN

- 40g [3 Tbsp] butter (or light olive oil to keep it vegan)
- 2 stems tender young rhubarb, sliced about 4mm [⅛in] thick
- 5 spring onions [scallions], sliced and white and green parts separated
- 1.2 litres [5 cups] good vegetable stock
- 2 tsp cornflour [cornstarch]
- a small handful of sugar snap peas, thickly sliced
- 70g [2½oz] asparagus tips, sliced on the diagonal
- 70g [2½oz] purple sprouting or long-stem broccoli, sliced lengthways though the stems if they are thick
- 70g [2½oz] baby broad [fava] beans (or 140g [5oz] broad beans, double podded)
- 70g [2½oz] peas (defrosted if frozen)
- 3 Tbsp snipped chives
- 3 Tbsp finely chopped parsley
- sea salt and freshly ground black pepper

For the mint & pistachio pesto:
- 25g [1oz] mint leaves
- 15g [½oz] pistachio nuts
- 3–4 Tbsp extra virgin olive oil
- 1 small garlic clove, chopped
- 1–2 Tbsp crème fraîche (optional)

Thai Broth

WITH CRAB, CHILLI & LIME DUMPLINGS

You can try sealing these little dumplings with a dainty, frilled, gyoza-esque seam if you wish, but you'll probably not have much luck with them holding themselves together. Using rice paper discs is far quicker than making the classic dumpling dough – and the result is much lighter – but it isn't quite as robust. While my stumpy little dumplings may not be the most elegant, rolling them up creates layers, which add strength to the fine rice paper and keep all that zingy filling contained once buoyed in the hot broth.

Put the stock in a saucepan and add the chilli, lemon grass and ginger. Pop a lid on the pan and bring to a simmer. Simmer for 20 minutes or so, until the Thai flavours have had a chance to infuse the stock.

Meanwhile, make the filling for the dumplings. Combine the crab, spring onions, chilli, lime zest and coriander leaves in a bowl and add a pinch of salt to season.

Fill a shallow bowl with warm water. Take a rice paper disc, dip it in warm water for a few seconds, then lay it on a board. Spoon a heaped teaspoon of the crab mixture to one side of the disc, and roll up, tucking in the sides as you go, as you would a spring roll. Repeat to roll 16 dumplings.

Strain the stock, discarding the aromatics, and return it to the pan. Add the fish sauce and a good squeeze of lime juice. Taste to check the seasoning – it might need salt, but often the fish sauce is very salty so you may not need to add any extra.

Add the dumplings to the pan, a few at a time, and cook for just a few seconds (30 maximum) to warm the crab through. Transfer them to shallow, warmed bowls.

Divide the broth between the bowls and add several Thai basil leaves to each bowl. Sprinkle with extra chilli, if using, and serve with lime wedges for squeezing.

SERVES 4 | DAIRY-FREE

1.2 litres [5 cups] chicken stock
½ red chilli, plus optional
    sliced chilli to serve
2 lemon grass stalks
4 thick slices fresh ginger
1 Tbsp Thai fish sauce
a squeeze of lime juice
a handful of Thai basil leaves
sea salt
lime wedges, to serve

For the dumplings:
250g [9oz] fresh crab meat
    (I use half brown, half
    white, but you could use all
    white meat if you prefer a
    more delicate crab flavour)
2 spring onions [scallions],
    very finely chopped
½ red chilli, very finely
    chopped
finely grated zest of ½ lime
a small handful of coriander
    [cilantro] leaves, chopped
16 rice paper wrappers (I use
    16cm [6¼in] discs)

Mussel & Samphire Broth

WITH LEMON GRASS

This is a shameless twist on a French staple, leaving out the conventional aromatics of thyme and bay and replacing them, perhaps brazenly, with a lemon grass stalk or two. As the cooking liquor has been increased in volume to make this more soupy than the classic moules marinières, a good fish stock is important; follow my recipe for fish stock on page 11 and make your own fresh, if you can.

Heat the butter and oil in a large saucepan set over low heat and add the shallots, lemon grass and garlic. Cook very gently for about 10 minutes, or until everything is well softened.

While the onions are softening, prepare the mussels. Wash and de-beard them. Discard any that are open and which don't close when given a sharp tap on the shell with the knife, as these may be dead.

Add the wine to the pan, turn up the heat to medium and let it reduce until the liquid has almost all gone. Add the stock to the pan, put the lid on and bring it to the boil, then reduce the heat so that the liquid is just simmering and add the mussels and the samphire. Cook for 3–4 minutes, until the mussels are cooked and have all opened and the samphire is tender.

Taste the broth and season with salt and pepper, then stir in the parsley just before serving. Ladle into shallow bowls, picking out and discarding any mussels that have not opened as you go, and serve with crusty bread.

SERVES 4

2 Tbsp butter
1 Tbsp olive oil
3 large echalion shallots, finely sliced
2 lemon grass stalks, very finely sliced (try and get it into shavings with a very sharp knife)
2 garlic cloves, finely chopped
1.2kg [2½lb] mussels
200ml [generous ¾ cup] white wine
1.4 litres [6 cups] good fish stock
100g [3½oz] samphire
a small handful of flat-leaf parsley leaves, roughly chopped
sea salt and freshly ground black pepper
crusty bread, to serve

Courgette & Caraway
WITH SMOKED SALMON & DILL SOURED CREAM

The list of ailments caraway is said to ease is impressive, but it's the flavour that generally gets my attention. I've left the seeds whole here, so that even once blended, you'll still get little hits of that lovely aniseedy fennel-like flavour, but you could grind the seeds more finely in a pestle and mortar first, if you prefer. Ever the Scandiphile, I've taken this north and added salmon and dill to the caraway. If you want to keep it vegetarian you can leave out the salmon, but I've personally never been known to turn down smoked salmon in my life.

Heat the oil in a large saucepan set over a low heat and sauté the onion, garlic and caraway seeds for 10 minutes, until the onion is soft and translucent. Add the courgettes, stock and rice and cook for 10–12 minutes, or until the rice is tender and the courgettes are softened.

Meanwhile, combine the soured cream and dill for serving and pop in the fridge until needed.

Once it's had its time, transfer the soup to a blender, add the 3 Tbsp soured cream and blitz until smooth. Add the herbs and blitz again briefly to just blend them in (it's nice to see flecks of them in the soup). Tip the soup back into the cleaned pan and season to taste with salt and pepper.

Ladle the soup into warmed bowls and top each serving with a spoonful of the dill soured cream. Finish with a scattering of salmon ribbons, a few snipped chives and a good grind of coarse black pepper.

SERVES 4

2 Tbsp olive oil
1 onion, diced
1 garlic clove, finely chopped
1¼ tsp caraway seeds
800g [1lb 12oz] courgettes
 [zucchini], sliced
800ml [3⅓ cups] vegetable
 stock
50g [⅓ cup] easy-cook rice
3 Tbsp soured cream
a small handful of chives,
 plus extra to serve
a small handful of dill fronds
sea salt and freshly ground
 black pepper

To serve:
4 Tbsp soured cream
2 Tbsp chopped dill
80g [3oz] smoked salmon,
 sliced into thin strips

Watermelon Gazpacho

WITH FETA, MINT & TOASTED SEEDS

Watermelon seeds are this season's bone broth (if you're late to this party, see page 52),
which was last season's maca, which replaced spirulina... ad infinitum. I'm not one for
superfood magic bullets: the seeds' inclusion here is simply in the spirit of mottainai
– waste not, want not. You don't want the black bits making your soup speckly or
getting between your teeth when you eat it, so as you're picking them out anyway,
they are pretty tasty when roasted and add another interesting texture. Skip them by
all means if you can't be bothered.

Put the watermelon, cucumber, tomatoes, garlic, onion, olive oil
and sherry vinegar in a liquidizer and blitz to a smooth, thick
liquid. Taste and season with salt and pepper. Tip the gazpacho
into a bowl or large jug and put in the fridge to chill for at least
2 hours before serving.

Meanwhile, preheat the oven to 180°C fan (350°F) Gas 4. Dry the
seeds that you have picked out of the melon really well with a
piece of kitchen paper, then tip them onto a baking sheet. Drizzle
with a little olive oil, sprinkle with salt and stir everything
together. Pop in the oven to roast for about 10–15 minutes until
crisp and toasty smelling.

To serve, give the chilled soup a really good stir and pour into
bowls. Top with a crumble of feta and a sprinkling of mint.
Finish with a few of the toasted seeds sprinkled over the top.

SERVES 4 | VEGETARIAN

600g [21oz] prepared
  watermelon (peeled and
  diced, black seeds picked
  out and reserved)
200g [7oz] peeled cucumber,
  cut into chunks
3 large tomatoes (about 300g/
  10½oz), deseeded and cut
  into chunks
1 small garlic clove
½ small red onion
3 Tbsp olive oil, plus extra
  to drizzle
½ Tbsp sherry vinegar
sea salt and freshly ground
  black pepper
100g [3½oz] Greek feta
  cheese, to serve (opt for a
  vegetarian alternative if
  necessary)
a small handful of mint
  leaves, finely shredded,
  to serve

Flexible Korean

BIBIM-BROTH

Korean cuisine has in its arsenal two amazing ingredients that will perk up a bowl of healthy, pure, crisp veggie soup without question – gochujang (a smoky red chilli paste) and the classic kimchi (fermented spicy vegetables). Armed with these, any veg that may have been hanging around in the fridge a bit long can be given a new lease of life. Follow the veggie suggestions below, or just add whatever you have to hand that appeals. A couple of tips here: a mandoline will speed up the process hugely; and buying your kombu from an Oriental supermarket will cost you far less than buying it from a health food store.

If the kombu is in large sheets, cut it into thick strips. Put it in a saucepan with the dried shiitake and cover with 1.2 litres [5 cups] cold water. Leave to soak for an hour.

Put the rice noodles in a large bowl and cover with warm water. Leave to soak for about 20 minutes, or until well softened.

Once the kombu and mushrooms have soaked, put the pan over low–medium heat and bring it up to a simmer slowly. Before it gets to boiling point, remove the pan from the heat and strain the dashi, discarding the kombu and mushrooms. Taste and season the stock with salt.

Divide the softened noodles between 4 bowls. Arrange piles of your chosen vegetables around the bowls, adding a spoonful each of kimchi and gochujang to each bowl, too.

Gently ladle the dashi evenly between the bowls, being careful not to ruin your arrangement, and serve with extra kimchi and gochujang on the side, and with chopsticks and a spoon for eating.

SERVES 4 | VEGETARIAN

10g [⅓oz] dried kombu
15g [½oz] dried shiitake
  mushrooms
200g [7oz] rice vermicelli
  noodles
4 Tbsp kimchi, plus extra
  to serve
4 tsp gochujang, plus extra
  to serve
sea salt

A selection of the below:
daikon radish, julienned or
  chopped into matchsticks
carrot, julienned or chopped
  into matchsticks
courgette [zucchini],
  spiralized, julienned or
  chopped into matchsticks
Chinese (or napa) cabbage,
  shredded
spinach, wilted
beansprouts
spring onions [scallions],
  sliced on the diagonal
mange tout [snow peas], sliced
  on the diagonal

Hong Kong Chicken Soup
WITH VEGGIE NOODLES

This is really a take on Singapore noodles, should Singaporeans have invented them. In fact, they are most likely a Cantonese creation and so attributing the inspiration for this pan-Asian soup to Hong Kong seems more accurate. But what HK cuisine shares with that of Singapore is a fusion of cultures that brings together Indian spices and Far East Asian seasonings. In an attempt to keep this a little lighter than the classic fried rice noodle dish, I have subbed in noodles made from carrot and courgette, for a refreshing, but still ridiculously comforting, take. If you don't have a spiralizer, just use a peeler to shave the carrot and courgette into flatter noodles.

Get everything chopped, spiralized and ready to go before you begin cooking, as that bit won't take long at all.

Heat the oil in a large saucepan set over low heat and add the onion, garlic, ginger and curry powder. Sauté them for about 8 minutes until the onion is well softened.

Meanwhile, divide the carrot and courgette noodles between 4 shallow bowls.

Turn up the heat to medium, add the cooked chicken, prawns, pepper and water chestnuts and cook for 3 minutes or so more until the veg are starting to soften.

Add the hot chicken stock to the pan, along with the oyster and soy sauces and the peas. Cook for just a couple of minutes until the peas are tender, but still bright green. You probably won't need seasoning as both sauces are quite salty.

Ladle the soup over the noodles in the bowls and serve.

SERVES 4 | DAIRY-FREE

2 Tbsp light oil, such as sunflower or groundnut
1 onion, sliced
2 garlic cloves, finely chopped
3cm [1¼in] piece of fresh ginger, finely chopped
1 Tbsp medium curry powder
1 large carrot, spiralized into noodles
1 large courgette [zucchini], spiralized into noodles
200g [7oz] cooked chicken, shredded
100g [3½oz] small peeled and cooked prawns [shrimp]
½ red [bell] pepper, sliced
1 x 225g [8oz] can sliced water chestnuts, drained
1.2 litres [5 cups] hot chicken stock (preferably homemade)
2 Tbsp premium-quality oyster sauce
2 Tbsp dark soy sauce
75g [½ cup] frozen peas, defrosted

Beef Bone Broth
WITH BLACK BEANS & CHIMICHURRI

There was a time not too long ago when various bone broths were being hailed as gut-healing miracle cures for the countless digestive complaints that plague us nowadays. There may or may not be solid medical or anecdotal evidence for this, but there definitely is something deeply satisfying about creating a delicious dinner out of what would ordinarily be discarded or given to the dog. It's great value, as a bag of marrow bones should cost you very little from your local butcher – and any ancillary digestive benefits are free. As a twist on the plethora of bone broth recipes already out there, I've given this one a Mendoza makeover and added chimichurri for a flavour boost along with black beans for ballast.

Preheat the oven to 190°C fan (375°F) Gas 5.

Put the bones into a large roasting pan and drizzle with a little oil. Roast for 30 minutes, then allow to cool in the pan. (You can skip this step if you don't have time but cooking the bones first does add flavour to the broth.)

Pick the bones out, leaving any fat in the roasting pan and put them in a large saucepan. Add the onion, leek, carrots, celery, bay leaves, peppercorns and herbs and cover with cold water. Bring to the boil, then lower the heat, skim any scum from the surface, and cover the pan with a lid. Cook, simmering gently, for 2 hours.

Meanwhile, put all the ingredients for the chimichurri in a mini chopper or the small bowl of a food processor and pulse to combine, leaving plenty of texture. Season to taste.

Drain the stock, discarding the vegetables and bones, and pour it into a clean pan. You can use the broth as it is, or keep to cooking it down to concentrate the flavour, if you wish.

When the stock is ready, tip in the beans, then taste and season with salt and black pepper.

Ladle the broth into bowls and top with a drizzle of the chimichurri, to serve.

SERVES 4 | VEGETARIAN

2kg [4½lb] beef bones
a drizzle of olive oil
1 onion, halved
1 leek, chopped into chunks
2 carrots, peeled and chopped
2 celery sticks, chopped
2 bay leaves
a few black peppercorns
a bunch of thyme and parsley stalks
1 x 400g [14oz] can black beans, drained and rinsed
sea salt and freshly ground black pepper

For the chimichurri:
½ (25g/1oz) pack flat-leaf parsley
½ (25g/1oz) pack coriander [cilantro]
½ (25g/1oz) pack oregano
3 Tbsp extra virgin olive oil
½ tsp crushed chilli flakes [red pepper flakes]
1½ Tbsp red wine vinegar
2 garlic cloves, finely chopped

Silken Broccoli & Ginger
WITH FIERY GINGER MATCHSTICKS

I've kept this a joyously quick-to-cook soup, not just for convenience but also out of a desire to keep the freshness of flavour. Despite the creaminess provided by the tofu (don't tell anyone who's likely to turn their nose up – it isn't even detectable once blended in), it still has a light lift from the Asian-inspired ingredients, and makes a refreshing change from all those broccoli and blue cheese soups – although, I don't deny that they have their place.

Heat the oil in a large saucepan set over low heat and sauté the spring onions, ginger and garlic for about 10 minutes until soft.

Meanwhile, chop the ginger for the matchsticks into fine strips with a sharp knife or using a julienne cutter or mandoline. Sprinkle a little cornflour onto a plate and toss the ginger matchsticks in it to lightly coat.

Heat a little oil in a small non-stick frying pan until hot. Scatter in a few of the ginger strips and fry, stirring regularly, for about 1 minute, or until golden brown. Remove from the pan with a slotted spoon and drain on a plate lined with kitchen paper. Repeat to fry the remaining matchsticks, then set aside.

Once the onions have had their 10 minutes, add the stock and bring to the boil. Add the broccoli, pop a lid on the pan and cook for 3 minutes until the broccoli is just cooked but still green. There's not a huge amount of liquid, so push the broccoli down into it and make sure you stir everything around a couple of times during cooking.

Transfer the soup to a blender and blitz until very smooth. Add the tofu and lemon zest, and season with salt, pepper and a squeeze of lemon juice. Blend again, then taste and adjust the seasoning, if you need to.

Pour the soup straight into 4 warmed bowls and top each with a little pile of ginger matchsticks, to serve.

SERVES 4 | VEGAN

2 Tbsp light oil (such as vegetable or sunflower)
6 fat spring onions [scallions], sliced
2 Tbsp peeled and finely chopped fresh ginger
1 garlic clove, chopped
800ml [3⅓ cups] homemade or light vegetable stock
1½ heads broccoli, finely chopped
150g [5½oz] firm silken tofu
grated zest of ½ lemon, plus a squeeze of juice
sea salt and freshly ground black pepper

For the fiery ginger matchsticks:
2cm [¾in] piece of fresh ginger, peeled
cornflour [cornstarch], for dusting
light oil, for shallow frying

Hearty &
WHOLESOME

Curried Paneer Soup

WITH SPINACH & SPLIT PEAS

This is a ridiculously sunny soup: perky spices, fresh green spinach, cheerfully yellow lentils and cheese fried to golden loveliness... I guess it's a sort of cross between a dhal and a saag paneer, only with everything loosened up a bit. I really like it brothy (it makes an uncommon contrast to what you'd usually imagine a dhal to be), but if that feels just too bizarre, feel free to stick an immersion blender in before you add the paneer and everything after. I wouldn't go too far though – just blend enough to thicken slightly, leaving a fair bit of texture.

Put the mustard and cumin seeds in a large saucepan and dry fry over a low heat for a couple of minutes until they start to pop and smell aromatic. Add 2 Tbsp of the oil along with the onion, garlic, garam masala and turmeric and continue to cook very gently for about 10 minutes until the onion is soft and translucent.

Add the split peas to the pan and stir to coat them in the spicy oil, then add the stock and cover the pan with a lid. Cook gently for about 40 minutes, or until the split peas are completely tender, but not breaking down.

Just before the soup has had its time, heat the remaining 1 Tbsp of oil in a non-stick (this is important, don't try and do it in any old pan) frying pan and set over high heat. Once hot, add the cubes of paneer and cook, stirring frequently, until they are golden all over. Tip them onto a plate lined with kitchen paper to drain.

Add the paneer, shredded spinach and coriander to the soup pan and stir in. Cook for just 1 minute or so, until the spinach has wilted down. Season with salt and pepper and a good squeeze of lemon juice and serve in warmed bowls.

SERVES 4 | VEGETARIAN

1 tsp mustard seeds
1 tsp cumin seeds
3 Tbsp light olive oil
1 onion, finely diced
2 garlic cloves, finely chopped
1 tsp garam masala
½ tsp ground turmeric
125g [⅔ cup] yellow split peas
1.2 litres [5 cups] vegetable stock
100g [3½oz] paneer cheese, cut into 5mm [¼in] dice (opt for a vegetarian alternative if necessary)
75g [1⅓ cups] spinach, shredded
a large handful of coriander [cilantro] leaves, roughly chopped
a good squeeze of lemon juice
sea salt and freshly ground black pepper

Very Herby Minestrone
WITH PLENTY OF PARMESAN

Who really needs another minestrone recipe? I was reluctant too, but as this soup is the very definition of nourishing, it seemed churlish to let popularity be a fair rationale for its exclusion. And the fact is, there is a reason it is so ubiquitous. You need to cook this in a big batch or you'll have a fridge full of lonely vegetable halves. Don't worry – it will keep happily, chilled, for a few days (even gets better after a day or two) and makes a satisfying packed lunch to pop in the office microwave with no need to bring bread. Don't let the long list of ingredients put you off – they are all cheap, and if you don't already have the different jars of dried herbs, a tablespoon of an Italian herb blend will do the trick. More Parmesan than you would ordinarily think prudent is a must for serving.

Heat the oil in a large saucepan over high heat and add the lardons. Fry for a few minutes until they are turning golden and crispy, then remove them to a plate with a slotted spoon, leaving the oil in the pan.

Turn the heat down to medium–low and add the diced onion. Cook for 5 minutes or so until starting to soften. Add the leek, celery, carrot, red pepper and garlic to the pan and sauté for about 5 more minutes until all the veg are beginning to soften, then add the courgette and chopped tomatoes and stir everything together.

Add the stock, tomato purée and dried herbs, cover the pan and turn the heat up to high to bring the liquid to the boil. Once boiling, turn it down to medium and simmer the soup for about 10 minutes, before adding the pasta and cavolo nero. Cook for a further 6–7 minutes, or until all the veg is tender and the pasta is cooked.

Add the cannellini beans and half of the fresh herbs and cook for just a couple of minutes until the beans are heated through. Season to taste with plenty of salt and pepper.

Ladle the soup into warmed bowls and serve sprinkled with the remaining fresh herbs and mountains of grated Parmesan.

SERVES 6–8

2 Tbsp olive oil
100g [3½oz] smoked bacon lardons or diced pancetta
1 large onion, finely diced
1 leek, finely sliced
1 celery stick, finely sliced
1 large carrot, peeled and diced
1 red [bell] pepper, diced
2 garlic cloves, chopped
1 courgette [zucchini], diced
2 x 400g [14oz] cans good-quality chopped tomatoes
1 litre [4¼ cups] chicken or vegetable stock
1 Tbsp tomato purée [paste]
1 tsp dried oregano
1 tsp dried thyme
½ tsp dried rosemary
125g [4½oz] tiny soup pasta shapes
100g [3½oz] cavolo nero, thick stalk removed and shredded
1 x 400g [14oz] can cannellini beans, drained and rinsed
1 (25g/1oz) bag basil, leaves shredded
1 (25g/1oz) bag oregano, leaves picked and roughly chopped
sea salt and freshly ground black pepper
plenty of finely grated Parmesan, to serve

Five-Spice Duck

WITH BUCKWHEAT NOODLES & BROCCOLI

This is like a duck pho – the meat is still pretty much raw in the middle when served and finishes cooking to rarest perfection in the hot broth. There are definitely two ways to do this, and one is most likely more flavoursome than the other, but then there are very few people who will feel like boiling up duck bones post 8P.M. on a school night and I am a realist. If you have a free-ish weekend afternoon, try making your own stock by following the meat stock recipe on page 9 and using duck carcasses, but you can get pretty delicious results from the below, too.

Heat the oil gently in a large saucepan and add the garlic and ginger. Cook for a few minutes, then add the spring onion whites, soy sauce, star anise, cinnamon and Sichuan pepper and cook for 2 more minutes, then add the stock. Let the pan bubble away gently while you sort out the duck.

Season the duck breasts with salt, then sprinkle over the 5-spice and rub it all over the duck pieces. Place them in a cold non-stick frying pan, skin side down, and turn the heat up to medium–high. Once the pan is hot, cook them for about 6–7 minutes, turning them over two-thirds of the way through, until the fat has rendered out of the skin and they are golden and browned on the outside (they will still be a little raw in the middle). Remove from the pan and leave to rest on a chopping board.

Add the noodles to the soup and cook for 3 minutes. Add the broccoli and cook for another 3 minutes, or until the noodles are cooked and the broccoli is tender but still has a bit of a bite. Taste the soup and add a little salt if needed, but it may not need it as the soy sauce is salty.

Ladle the soup into bowls. Slice the duck very thinly with a sharp knife and share between the bowls. Finish with a sprinkle of spring onion greens and a little more Sichuan pepper.

SERVES 4 | DAIRY-FREE

2 tsp toasted sesame oil

2 large garlic cloves, sliced

2.5cm [1in] piece of fresh ginger, peeled and cut into matchsticks

1 small bunch of spring onions [scallions], about 8, sliced on the diagonal and white and green parts separated

2 Tbsp dark soy sauce

2 star anise

1 cinnamon stick

1 tsp Sichuan peppercorns, plus a little extra to sprinkle

1.5 litres [6½ cups] good chicken or duck stock

2 duck breasts

2 tsp Chinese 5-spice powder

120g [4½oz] buckwheat noodles (100% if you can find them)

160g [5½oz] Tenderstem broccoli

sea salt

Turkey Meatballs & Kale
WITH SWEET POTATO & SHALLOTS

There's a bit of groundwork to be done here, but it's worth the effort. If you want to cut corners, you could use cut-up sausages instead of making the meatballs, but it won't be as healthy as using minced turkey, or probably as tasty.

Start by making the meatballs. Heat the oil in a small frying pan over a low heat and sauté the onion and garlic gently for 8–10 minutes until really softened and tender. Once softened, turn off the heat and leave to cool in the pan.

Tip the minced turkey into a mixing bowl and add the cooled onion mixture and all the remaining meatball ingredients. Using your hands, massage the mixture together to make sure everything is really well combined. Divide the mixture into 20 rough balls, place them on a plate and cover with cling film [plastic wrap], and chill in the fridge for an hour or so (or longer – you can do this well in advance). Once cold the meatballs will be easier to shape into neater balls, and you can use a dusting of flour on your hands if that helps, too.

Heat the oil in a non-stick frying pan set over medium heat. Fry the shallots for 6–7 minutes, or until caramelized and turning golden, then tip them into a large saucepan, holding the oil back in the frying pan. Turn the heat up to high and let the frying pan get really hot, then add the meatballs and fry, turning frequently, until browned on the outside (you may need to do in batches). Tip those into the saucepan also.

Add the stock, sweet potato and thyme to the saucepan, pop a lid on and bring the liquid to the boil. Once boiling, turn the heat down and simmer for about 15 minutes, or until the sweet potato is tender. Add the kale, Worcestershire sauce and mustard and cook for another 2–3 minutes until the kale has wilted down.

Taste and season well with salt and black pepper, then ladle into warmed bowls, dividing the meatballs evenly between the bowls.

SERVES 4 | DAIRY-FREE

2 Tbsp olive oil
200g [7oz] small shallots, peeled and sliced in half
1.25 litres [5 cups] chicken stock
2 small or 1 large sweet potato (about 275g/10oz), peeled and diced into 1cm [½in] cubes
leaves from 3 thyme sprigs
100g [3½oz] kale, tough stalks removed and ripped into bite-sized pieces
1 Tbsp Worcestershire sauce
2 tsp wholegrain mustard

For the meatballs:
1 Tbsp olive oil
1 small red onion, finely diced
1 large garlic clove, crushed
250g [9oz] minced [ground] turkey thighs
2 tsp finely chopped fresh sage leaves
2 tsp finely chopped fresh rosemary needles
50g [1 cup] fresh brown breadcrumbs
1 egg
½ tsp ground allspice
½ Tbsp sea salt flakes
½ tsp black pepper
plain [all-purpose] flour, to dust (if needed)

Spinach & Chickpea

WITH CHORIZO & A HINT OF CINNAMON

Credit must go to Rick Stein for the inspiration for this soup. A long time ago, I was cooked a meal with these flavours from one of his wonderful books; this soup is an homage to that dish, which has stayed with me many years later. I can't remember the recipe in detail, and nor would I wish to plagiarize, but the titular ingredients featured and formed a winning combination. While there are undoubtedly myriad recipes for Spanish chorizo and chickpea soups, it's the addition of a gentle hint of cinnamon that gives this its staying power.

Heat the oil in a large saucepan set over a high heat and add the chorizo. Cook for about 3 minutes, stirring frequently, until it is beginning to brown and release its oils.

Turn the heat down to low and add the onion, garlic, bay leaf, thyme and cinnamon stick. Cook for about 10 minutes, stirring frequently, until the onions have softened.

Add the stock, pop a lid on the pan and turn up the heat to bring the liquid to a boil. Once boiling, lower the heat to medium to keep the soup at a simmer. Add the tomatoes and chickpeas and allow everything to bubble away for about 10 minutes to infuse the flavours.

Fish out the cinnamon stick halves and bay leaf and discard them. To thicken, transfer a few ladles of the soup (about one-quarter of the total volume) to a food processor and blitz it until smooth. Return the blended soup to the pan. (You could also just blitz briefly with an immersion blender to part-blend, if you prefer a chunkier texture.) Add the spinach and cook for a minute or so until it has wilted down. Taste and season well with salt and pepper, then ladle into warmed bowls to serve.

SERVES 4

1 Tbsp olive oil
125g [4½oz] chorizo, diced
1 large onion, finely sliced
2 garlic cloves, finely chopped
1 bay leaf
1 thyme sprig
1 long, chunky cinnamon
 stick, snapped in half
1 litre [4¼ cups] chicken stock
3 large tomatoes (about
 350g/12oz in total),
 deseeded and diced
1 x 400g [14oz] can chickpeas
 [garbanzo beans], drained
120g [2½ cups] fresh spinach,
 roughly sliced
sea salt and freshly ground
 black pepper

Kosheri-ish Soup

WITH BARBERRIES & CRISPY ONIONS

I used to believe that if you needed a bowl of something truly comforting and restorative, you had to choose between pasta, or rice, or dhal, or any other complex carb for that matter. And then I discovered kosheri and realized that I was, quite frankly, an amateur. Why choose merely one when you can take a leaf out of the Egyptians' book and stick all three in together?

Heat the oil in a large saucepan set over low heat, add the sliced onions, and cook for 10 minutes until softened. Add the garlic and spices and cook for another 10 minutes until the onions are really beginning to caramelize and turn a light golden brown.

Add the butter and let it melt, then add the red lentils and rice and stir them around to coat in the spicy butter. Add the stock, cover the pan with a lid and turn the heat up to high to bring the soup to the boil, then reduce the heat back to medium and simmer for 10 minutes.

Add the pasta and cook for another 7–8 minutes, until it is tender. Turn off the heat and stir in the dried barberries and lemon zest, then taste and season well with salt and black pepper and a good squeeze of lemon juice.

Ladle the soup into warmed bowls and serve with a sprinkling of chopped parsley and tons of crispy fried onions piled on top.

SERVES 4–6 | VEGAN

2 Tbsp olive oil
2 onions, finely sliced
3 garlic cloves, finely chopped
1½ tsp ground cinnamon
¾ tsp freshly grated nutmeg
1 tsp ground cumin
30g [2 Tbsp] butter (leave this
    out to keep it vegan)
75g [⅓ cup] red lentils
40g [¼ cup] white basmati
    rice
1.3 litres [generous 5 cups]
    vegetable stock
30g [1oz] vermicelli or angel
    hair pasta, broken into
    2.5cm [1in] lengths
30g [1oz] dried barberries
    (available in most Asian
    grocers – don't even think
    about skipping them)
zest of ½ small lemon
a good squeeze of lemon juice
sea salt and freshly ground
    black pepper
roughly chopped flat-leaf
    parsley, to serve
plenty of crispy fried onions,
    to serve

Polish Sausage
WITH CABBAGE & MUSHROOMS

With its intriguing blend of Gothic and Renaissance architecture, Krakow's town square blanketed in a thick layer of February snow is one of the most beautiful sights I have ever seen. But it's not for the faint hearted – stinging Siberian winds whip around the buildings and a post-wander warm-up was definitely required. So it's fortunate that the Poles have comfort food pegged, and bigos (hunter's stew) is everything you could hope for on a wintry day. Polish kabernos sausage has an amazing, distinctive smoky flavour that makes it the star of this soup, which is roughly based on that classic Polish dish.

Put the dried mushrooms in a bowl, cover with about 100ml [⅓ cup] hot water, and leave to soak.

Heat the oil in a large saucepan over high heat and add the lardons. Fry them for a few minutes until they are turning golden and the fat is rendering out, then add the sausages and cook for another couple of minutes.

Turn the heat down to low–medium, add the onion, mushrooms and caraway seeds, and cook for about 8 minutes more until the onions are softening and the mushrooms are picking up some colour. Add the cabbage and juniper berries and cook for a further 5 minutes, until the cabbage is well wilted.

Meanwhile, strain the dried mushrooms, reserving the soaking water, and chop them. Add them to the pan along with the apple. Add the mushroom soaking water too, pouring it in slowly and discarding any gritty looking liquid at the bottom of the jug. Cook for 1–2 minutes until the liquid has reduced, then add the beef stock.

Turn the heat up to bring the liquid to a boil, then once boiling, turn it back down so that the soup is simmering. Cover the pan and leave to bubble away for 30 minutes, until the cabbage is really soft and all the flavours have got to know each other.

Taste and season with salt and plenty of pepper, then ladle into 4 warmed bowls to serve.

SERVES 4

10g [⅓oz] dried mushrooms
1 Tbsp olive oil
125g [4½oz] smoked bacon
    lardons or pancetta
100g [3½oz] kabernos sausage,
    sliced
1 large onion, finely sliced
150g [2 cups] baby button
    mushrooms (chestnut if
    possible), quartered
½ tsp caraway seeds
½ small white cabbage, cored
    and finely shredded (about
    150g [5½oz] prepared
    weight)
8 juniper berries, crushed
1 apple, grated (leave the
    skin on)
1.2 litres [5 cups] beef stock
sea salt and freshly ground
    black pepper

Chunky Creole Fish Stew

WITH PEPPER & TOMATO

The lengthy ingredient list here speaks for the vibrancy of Creole food and the melting pot of cultures it incorporates; but don't let that fool you into thinking this is complicated. This is one-pot cooking at its best – inviting, colourful and relaxed, and the serving style should roughly follow suit; just pop a pan of this on the table with chunks of crusty bread and let everyone dig in. A welcoming warmth from the cayenne adds authenticity, but the heat shouldn't be so far up the Scoville scale that it distracts from the delicate taste of the seafood. By the way, don't worry about spending lots of money on expensive fresh crab meat – canned is fine as it will happily disperse itself into the soup base and provide a deep ambient shellfishy flavour.

Heat the oil and butter in a large saucepan over medium–low heat and sweat the onion and celery for 7–8 minutes until well softened. Add the garlic and peppers and continue to cook for a few minutes more until softened.

Add the stock, passata, bay leaf, spices and dried herbs and cook for about 15 minutes until all the vegetables are tender. Add the tomatoes and cook for about 3 minutes, then add the all the fish and cook for another 3 minutes or until the fish is just cooked.

Ladle the soup into 4 shallow bowls, being careful to divide the lumps of fish and prawns reasonably evenly, and enjoy with fresh crusty bread, to mop up all the juices.

SERVES 4–6

2 Tbsp oil
1 Tbsp butter
1 large onion, finely diced
2 celery sticks, finely sliced
3 large garlic cloves, finely chopped
1 red [bell] pepper, diced
1 green [bell] pepper, diced
1 litre [4¼ cups] fish stock
200ml [¾ cup] passata [strained tomatoes]
1 bay leaf
1 tsp cayenne pepper (or more to taste)
1 tsp sweet smoked paprika (pimentón dulce)
½ tsp black peppercorns, ground in a pestle and mortar
1 tsp sea salt
1 tsp dried thyme
1 tsp dried oregano
250g [9oz] fresh tomatoes, cut into chunks
300g [10½oz] white fish, such as cod, cut into 2.5cm [1in] chunks
200g [7oz] large prawns [shrimp], shelled weight (keep the shells for stock)
1 x 170g [6oz] can lump crab meat
fresh crusty bread, to serve

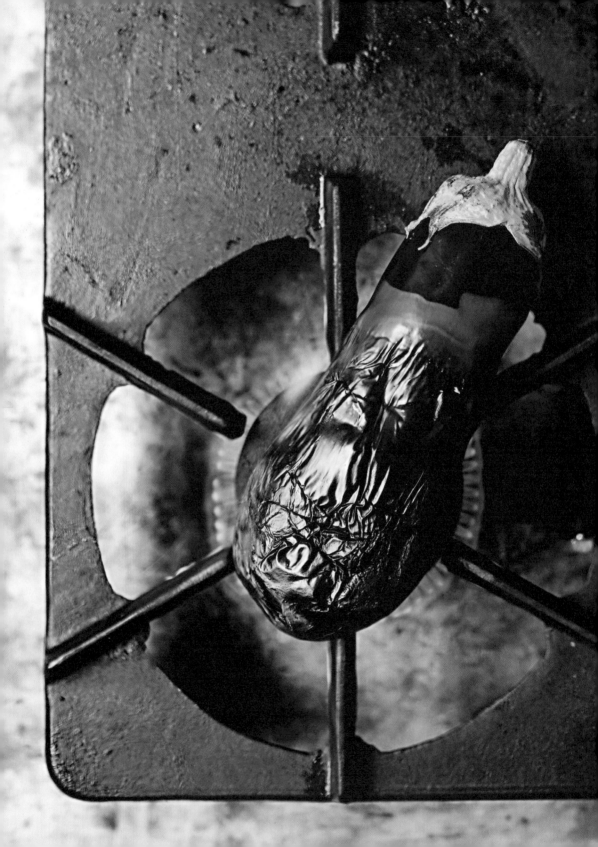

Smoked Aubergine

WITH PUY LENTILS & CARAMELIZED RED ONION

This soup certainly isn't going to win any beauty awards – it's too uniformly brown to elicit any genuine delight based on looks alone – but sometimes it really is what's on the inside that counts and, platitudes aside, this is seriously delicious. If you like anything with a smoky flavour, it's a great way to prepare aubergines, and they'll lend themselves to anything vaguely Middle Eastern in flavour, so try them as a topping for the Kosheri-ish Soup with Barberries & Crispy Onions on page 68.

Start with the onions. Heat the oil in a large saucepan and add the onions, balsamic and a good pinch of salt. Cook over a low heat, stirring frequently, until the onions are caramelized and brown. This could take a good 25 minutes, but don't rush it.

While the onions are cooking, put the aubergine over the naked gas hob flame (or you could use a blowtorch or a very hot electric grill [broiler] for this) and cook for 10–15 minutes, turning regularly with tongs, until the skin is charred and cracking all over and the flesh feels soft and squidgy. It might make a bit of a mess, but it's easy to wipe up and is worth it for the intense flavour. Once softened, move the aubergine to a plate and leave until cool enough to handle.

Once the onions are cooked, stir in the garlic and lentils and cook for a couple more minutes. Add the stock, along with the thyme, rosemary and bay leaf, cover the pan with a lid and cook for 20 minutes, or until the lentils are tender.

Meanwhile, remove the skin from the aubergine, removing as much of the charred flakes as possible. Do this over a plate as juices will run out as you do it and you'll want to collect these. Discard the burnt skin and chop the soft flesh into smallish dice.

Add the aubergine to the pan along with any juices that have accumulated on the plate. Add the mushroom ketchup, then taste and season (generously) with salt and pepper, and more mushroom ketchup, if wished.

Ladle into 4 warmed bowls (pulling out the thyme stalks as you come across them) to serve.

SERVES 4–6 | VEGAN

2 Tbsp olive oil
2 red onions, finely sliced
2 tsp balsamic vinegar
1 large aubergine [eggplant]
2 garlic cloves, finely sliced
120g [²⁄₃ cup] Puy lentils
1.2 litres [5 cups] hot vegetable stock
2 bushy sprigs of thyme
1 rosemary stalk, needles picked and finely chopped
1 bay leaf
1 Tbsp mushroom ketchup (such as Geo Watkins), or more to taste
sea salt and freshly ground black pepper

Slow-Cooked Lamb

WITH TOMATO, FENNEL SEED & FARRO

I used to make a lamb ragù based roughly on this, using minced meat instead of shanks, but I see no reason not to loosen it up a bit as – to my mind – lamb, tomato and fennel seeds do form a sort of flavour holy trinity that should be exploited as often as possible. Cooking the shanks long and slow results in an intense base stock that gives the soup a marvellously deep flavour, but you'll need to start it the day before.

Put all the stock ingredients in a large saucepan (a stock pan if you have one) and cover with about 2 litres [2 quarts] of cold water. Put a lid on the pan and bring to the boil over medium heat. Skim any foam from the surface, then lower the heat to low–medium and cook, loosely covered, for 2 hours, skimming occasionally if more foam is gathering on the top.

When the 2 hours is up, allow to cool a little, then strain out the vegetables and meat and reserve the stock. Discard the vegetables. Once cool enough to handle, strip the lamb from the bones, rip or cut it into small pieces and set aside (in the fridge if not using straight away). Measure the stock and, if you need to, reduce it down in a clean saucepan over medium heat until you have about 1 litre (4¼ cups). Allow to cool completely until set by the natural gelatine in the meat (it's best to make this the day before), then scrape off and discard any fat from the top.

For the soup, put the oil from the can of anchovies into a large saucepan set over low–medium heat. Add the onion, celery and carrot and cook for about 5 minutes until starting to soften. Add the anchovies, fennel seeds and garlic and cook gently for another 5 minutes or so until everything is smelling aromatic.

Add the red wine and cook until it has reduced to about half its original volume, then add the lamb stock, tomatoes, oregano, tomato purée and farro and cook for 20 minutes, or until the farro is tender but still has a slight bite. Add the shredded lamb to the soup and leave to just heat through. Taste and season well with salt and black pepper, then ladle into warmed bowls and serve.

SERVES 6 | DAIRY-FREE

For the stock:
2 lamb shanks
1 large onion, halved
1 large carrot, peeled and chopped into chunks
1 large leek, chopped into chunks
2 large celery sticks, chopped into chunks
a bouquet garni made of parsley stalks, thyme sprig and fresh bay leaf
a few black peppercorns

For the soup:
50g [2oz] can anchovies in oil, drained but oil reserved
1 onion, finely sliced
1 celery stick, finely sliced
1 large carrot, finely diced
2 tsp fennel seeds
2 large garlic cloves, crushed
150ml [⅔ cup] red wine
2 x 400g [14oz] cans good-quality chopped tomatoes
1 tsp dried oregano
1 Tbsp tomato purée [paste]
75g [2½oz] dried farro grain
sea salt and freshly ground black pepper

Brussels Sprout & Pancetta

WITH RED RICE

If you were planning to skip this page, haunted by the memory of Gran's slimy brown sulphurous sprouts, boiled to oblivion, don't. Sautéeing the Brussels rather than stewing them in the stock brings out the best of their flavour, which is helped along with smoky pancetta (make a special trip to a good deli for this – you require something that comes wrapped lovingly in wax paper) and nutty red rice. And if you want to recreate a soupy version of your favourite Christmas side, just chuck in a few chopped roasted chestnuts and/or dried cranberries.

Heat the oil in a large saucepan set over high heat and add the pancetta. Fry it for a few minutes until it is turning golden and crispy and the fat has rendered out. Carefully tip most of the fat into a large non-stick frying pan and set that aside.

Lower the heat under the saucepan to low and add the onion and garlic to the pan. Sauté for about 8 minutes until the onions are soft and translucent. Add the chicken stock and rice to the pan and cover with a lid. Raise the heat to high to bring the liquid to the boil, then lower it to medium and leave to simmer for 25–30 minutes, or until the rice is cooked and tender.

Towards the end of the cooking time, heat the reserved oil in the frying pan set over high heat and add the shredded sprouts. Sauté for about 4 minutes, stirring frequently, until the sprouts are softened and beginning to brown.

Once the rice is tender, add the sprouts to the soup along with the nutmeg, mushroom ketchup, if using, and some seasoning. Taste and adjust the seasoning if needed, then ladle into warmed bowls to serve.

SERVES 4 | DAIRY-FREE

2 Tbsp olive oil
160g [5½oz] best smoky
  pancetta, rind removed
  and diced
1 large onion, diced
2 garlic cloves, finely diced
1.4 litres [6 cups] good
  chicken stock (preferably
  homemade)
75g [½ cup] Camargue red rice
250g [9oz] Brussels sprouts,
  shredded very finely
¾ tsp freshly grated nutmeg
2 tsp mushroom ketchup
  (such as Geo Watkins)
sea salt and freshly ground
  black pepper

Freekeh & Soy

WITH BLACKENED SPRING ONION & CASHEW

*Hunches in the kitchen should generally not be ignored – this soup is proof of that.
It's a ragtag jumble of ingredients united by a vague feeling that it would somehow be
better than the sum of its parts; it was. Serve it with a fork so you can twist the spring
onions up against your spoon, spaghetti-style.*

Heat the oil in a large saucepan set over a low heat and add the
onion, carrot, celery and garlic. Sauté gently for about 10 minutes
until everything is softening. Add the freekeh and stir in, then
add the soy sauce and cook for a couple of minutes, or until the
liquid has reduced right down. Add the stock and increase the
heat to medium–high until the soup is boiling, then lower the
heat so the soup is simmering, pop a lid on the pan and leave
to cook for 15 minutes or so until the freekeh is tender.

Meanwhile, trim the tops off the spring onions and just trim
enough of the bottoms so that you remove the hairy bits, but
there's still enough root to keep them together. Slice them in half
lengthways and drizzle with a little olive oil. Brush it all over the
onions so they are lightly coated.

Preheat a griddle pan until very hot and add half of the spring
onions. Cook for a couple of minutes on each side, turning with
tongs, until they are starting to go dark brown in places, but
there's still plenty of green to be seen. Remove with the tongs
and cook the second half of the spring onions.

Once the soup has had its time, taste it and season with salt (be
modest here as the soy is very salty) and pepper. Ladle it into
warmed bowls and top each bowl with a quarter of the charred
onions. Sprinkle over the cashews to serve.

SERVES 4 | DAIRY-FREE

2 Tbsp olive oil, plus extra
   to drizzle
1 onion, finely diced
1 carrot, finely diced
1 celery stick, finely diced
1 garlic clove, finely chopped
85g [3oz] greenwheat freekeh
75ml [5 Tbsp] dark soy sauce
1.2 litres [5 cups] rich chicken
   or vegetable stock
16 large spring onions
   [scallions]
sea salt and freshly ground
   black pepper
60g [½ cup] roasted, salted
   cashews, roughly chopped,
   to serve

Pig Cheek & Celeriac

WITH PEARL BARLEY, SAGE & APPLE

If, when the Sunday roast chicken is being carved, you're generally found eyeing up the legs, consider the cheeks used here as the piggy equivalent. They are the dark meat of the animal – juicy and, in my opinion, much more flavoursome than most other cuts. They are often ground into mince before they make it to supermarket shelves, but you can usually get them from your local butcher if you ask nicely. Cooked slowly until falling-apart tender and teamed with some complementary veggies and herbs, they make a great base for a hearty soup.

Heat half the oil in a large saucepan set over high heat. Fry half of the pigs' cheeks until taking on some colour. Transfer the meat to a plate with a slotted spoon, add the remaining oil, and fry the other half of the meat. Remove that from the pan too, then turn the heat down to low.

Add the onion and garlic to the pan (add a tiny splash of the stock if there's not enough oil left to stop them sticking). Cook for 10 minutes until well softened. Add the meat back in (along with any juices that may have collected on the plate) with the sage and stir together, then tip in the stock and add the bay leaves. Put a lid on the pan and increase the heat to bring the liquid to the boil, then lower the heat until it is just simmering and leave to bubble away for 1 hour.

After an hour, add the pearl barley and celeriac and cook for 20 minutes more. Add the apple and cook for a final 5–10 minutes until the vegetables and the pearl barley are tender and the apple is softened, but not breaking down. Taste and season with salt and black pepper.

Ladle the soup into warmed bowls and serve.

SERVES 4 | DAIRY-FREE

2 Tbsp olive oil
400g [14oz] pigs' cheeks, diced
1 large onion, diced
1 large garlic clove, finely
 chopped
8 sage leaves, shredded
1.2 litres [5 cups] chicken stock
2 fresh bay leaves
75g [½ cup] pearl barley
½ small celeriac [celery root],
 peeled and diced (about
 250g/9oz prepared weight)
1 large pink-skinned apple,
 cored and diced (leave the
 skin on for a bit of colour)
sea salt and freshly ground
 black pepper

Moroccan-Spiced Chicken
WITH OLIVE, PRESERVED LEMON & COUSCOUS

I've a particular fondness for this soupy invention, primarily because it has nursed me through the winter's worst sniffles. A sort of loosened-up version of a tagine, the traditional couscous accompaniment is obligingly built in, and it packs in those healing, anti-inflammatory spices so there's plenty going on, flavour wise; it'll perk up ailing taste buds if nothing else. I'm not claiming to have cracked the cure for the common cold, but perhaps living through one needn't be so miserable after all?

Put the saffron in a small bowl and cover with a splash of warm water. Leave to soak.

Heat the oil in a large saucepan set over high heat and fry the chicken for a few minutes, stirring frequently, until it's beginning to brown. Turn the heat down to low–medium and add the onion, garlic and ginger and cook for about 8 minutes, or until the onion is really soft. Add the ground coriander, cumin and turmeric, stir in, and cook for another 1 minute or so until they are smelling aromatic.

Add the stock, turn the heat up to high and bring the liquid to the boil, then lower the heat to medium so the soup is simmering. Add the saffron and its soaking water, and the couscous, olives and preserved lemon. Pop a lid on the pan, and cook for about 8 minutes, or until the couscous is tender.

Season well with salt and pepper and stir in the parsley just before serving.

SERVES 4 | DAIRY-FREE

a pinch of saffron threads

2 Tbsp olive oil

300g [10½oz] skinned and boneless chicken thighs, finely sliced

1 large onion, finely diced

2 large garlic cloves, finely chopped

2.5cm [1in] piece of fresh ginger, peeled and finely chopped

1½ tsp ground coriander

1 tsp ground cumin

½ tsp ground turmeric

1.2 litres [5 cups] chicken stock

80g [3oz] wholewheat giant couscous

50g [⅓ cup] green olives, sliced

1 small preserved lemon, flesh discarded and skin finely chopped

a large handful of flat-leaf parsley leaves, roughly chopped

sea salt and freshly ground black pepper

Mixed Wild Mushroom

WITH TARRAGON & PEARLED SPELT

Punchy wild mushrooms and the liquorice undertones of tarragon make a pretty good flavour match in this autumnal broth, while spelt provides a satisfying bite. This recipe came to me while watching the closing minutes of Phantom Thread, and while I can't promise a bowl of it will truly tame an artistic temperament, it will have a good go at quietening any early-onset winter blues. Just make sure you're on good terms with your local greengrocer.

Put the dried mushrooms in a small bowl and cover with water (about 100ml/⅓ cup). Leave to soak while you ready the other soup bits.

Heat the oil in a large saucepan over a low heat and add the onion and garlic. Cook gently for about 10 minutes until soft and beginning to caramelize. Add the butter to the pan and let it melt, then add the fresh mushrooms and increase the heat slightly to medium. Cook for 5 minutes until the mushrooms are wilted and beginning to take on some colour.

Meanwhile, strain the dried mushrooms, reserving the soaking water, and chop them roughly.

Add the stock, star anise and spelt to the pan, Add the chopped soaked mushrooms along with the soaking water, slowly, discarding any gritty bits at the bottom. Cook for 15–20 minutes until the spelt is cooked but still has a bite.

Add a splash of Madeira to the pan and season well with salt and pepper. Stir in the herbs and serve immediately, topped with a crumble of goat's cheese and a sprinkle of walnuts, if wished.

SERVES 4 | VEGETARIAN

15g [½oz] dried porcini
  mushrooms
1 Tbsp walnut or olive oil
1 large red onion, finely sliced
2 garlic cloves, finely sliced
1 Tbsp butter (or use a little
  more oil if you want to keep
  it vegan)
300g [10½oz] wild
  mushrooms, sliced
1.2 litres [5 cups] good
  vegetable stock
1 star anise
100g [⅓ cup] pearled spelt
a good splash of Madeira wine
a small bunch of flat-leaf
  parsley, roughly chopped
a small bunch of tarragon,
  roughly chopped
soft goat's cheese, to serve
  (optional)
toasted walnuts, roughly
  chopped, to serve (optional)

Wintery Roots & Hardy Herbs
WITH CHESTNUTS

This is at heart a fancy Scotch broth, minus the lamb. In its place – and also doing a sterling job of standing in for the pearl barley – are sweet, meaty chestnuts. They provide a different but complementary texture and add a flash of creamy richness in what's essentially a peasant-style stew. While their earthiness chimes with the veggies and stops them feeling out of place, they still manage to proffer a pleasing punctuation mark in a bowl of modest roots.

Heat the oil in a large saucepan set over low heat and sauté the onion for 5 minutes. Add the carrot, parsnip, swede, leek, celery and garlic and cook for another 5 minutes. Add the vegetable stock along with all the herbs and bring to the boil. Lower the heat so that the liquid is simmering and cook for 15–20 minutes until the vegetables are almost tender.

Mix the cornflour with a splash of water, then tip this into the pan and cook for another 5 minutes until the soup has thickened a little and the vegetables are perfectly cooked. Stir in the chestnuts and let them heat through for a couple of minutes. Add the mustard, taste and season well with salt and pepper.

Ladle into warmed bowls to serve.

SERVES 4 | VEGETARIAN

2 Tbsp rapeseed [canola] or olive oil
1 onion, diced
1 carrot, peeled and diced
1 parsnip, peeled and diced
½ small swede [rutabaga] (about 200g/7oz), peeled and diced
1 leek, sliced
1 celery stick, sliced
2 garlic cloves, finely chopped
1.2 litres [5 cups] vegetable stock
leaves from a small bunch of thyme sprigs, stripped from stalks
needles from a bushy rosemary sprig, chopped
about 8 large sage leaves, shredded
2 bay leaves
1 Tbsp cornflour [cornstarch]
90g [3oz] roasted chestnuts (from a pre-cooked pouch or can), roughly diced
½ tsp wholegrain mustard
sea salt and freshly ground black pepper

Slow-Baked Greek Bean

WITH HALLOUMI CROUTONS

You'll get a generous casserole dish full of this, but if you're going to go to the trouble of soaking, shelling and slow-cooking beans, you may as well make the effort worthwhile. And it's not without its perks – the gentle monotony of peeling beans was surely the world's therapy before we invented life coaches and bubble wrap.

Put the beans in a bowl and cover with cold water. Leave them to soak for a day or so, until the skins are really loose and easy to remove. Pop them out of their little white jackets and set aside.

Preheat the oven to 160°C fan (325°F) Gas 3.

Heat the oil in a large casserole over low heat and sauté the onion and garlic gently for about 10 minutes until softened and translucent. Add a can of tomatoes, then refill the can with water and tip it into the pan. Add the second can of tomatoes and another 2 cans of water, then add the shelled beans, jelly stock, tomato purée and three-quarters of the oregano.

Pop the lid on the casserole and bring the liquid to a boil on the hob. Put in the oven and bake for 3 hours, stirring once an hour or so, until the beans are really tender. They will break down into shards, rather than the mush you would get from the canned variety, but should still be very soft. Remove the pan from the oven and stir in the sugar, sherry vinegar and the remaining oregano. Season really well with salt and pepper (the beans will take quite a bit of salt).

Once the soup is ready, prepare the halloumi. Heat a drizzle of oil in a non-stick frying pan over medium heat and fry the halloumi cubes for 4–5 minutes, turning frequently with tongs, until it is picking up some colour on all sides and feels soft.

Ladle the soup into bowls and top with the halloumi dice, a good grind of coarse black pepper and a few more oregano leaves.

SERVES 6 | VEGETARIAN

250g [1⅔ cups] dried butter [lima] beans
2 Tbsp olive oil, plus a drizzle for cooking the halloumi
1 large onion, finely diced
3 large garlic cloves, finely chopped
2 x 400g [14oz] cans chopped tomatoes
1 jelly vegetable stock pot
1½ heaped Tbsp tomato purée [paste]
20g [¾oz] fresh oregano, leaves roughly chopped, plus extra to serve
½ tsp dark brown sugar
1 tsp sherry vinegar
sea salt and freshly ground black pepper
1 x 250g [9oz] pack of halloumi, cut into 1.5cm [⅝in] cubes (opt for a vegetarian alternative if necessary)

Venison & Beluga Lentils

WITH CHERRIES & JUNIPER

Soup frequently gets under-sold as a cheap convenience food. Of course, it clearly can be, and many of the recipes in this book will challenge even toast for that coveted high-satisfaction-to-low-effort ratio. But sometimes you want a bit more: the (eponymously) literal caviar of the pulse clan; a deer that you'd like to imagine has spent its days trotting happily through a leafy royal park; a full-bodied red wine of a good vintage; plump, tangy cherries to add a crucial final bite of sweetness; and a carefree hour of tranquil, stove-top bubbling.

Heat ½ Tbsp of the oil in a large saucepan set over very high heat and fry half the venison until browned all over. Remove the meat with a slotted spoon, then add ½ Tbsp more oil and the remaining venison and repeat, then set the meat aside on a plate.

Add the remaining 1 Tbsp oil to the saucepan, turn the heat down to low and add the onions, balsamic vinegar and a good pinch of salt. Cook for a good 25 minutes or so until the onions are caramelizing and going sticky.

Meanwhile, cover the porcini with about 100ml [⅓ cup] hot water and leave to soak for 15 minutes. Drain the mushrooms over a jug, retaining the liquid, and roughly chop them.

Add the garlic and crushed juniper berries to the onions and cook for another 3 minutes or so, then add the wine and cook until it has reduced and there's only a couple of tablespoons of liquid left in the pan. Add the porcini soaking water, pouring it in slowly and discarding any gritty looking liquid at the bottom of the jug. Again, cook until the liquid has reduced right down.

Add the stock to the pan, along with the rosemary, bay leaf, chopped porcini and the browned venison. Put the lid on and simmer for at least 1 hour over a low heat, or until the meat is very tender.

Add the lentils, cherries and cavolo nero to the pan and cook for a couple of minutes to warm them all through. Taste for seasoning and add to your liking – it will probably need a fair bit – then ladle into warmed bowls to serve.

SERVES 4–6 | DAIRY-FREE

2 Tbsp olive oil

300g [10½oz] diced venison shoulder

2 red onions, finely sliced

1 Tbsp good-quality balsamic vinegar

10g [⅓oz] dried porcini mushrooms

2 garlic cloves, finely chopped

8 juniper berries, roughly crushed with the side of a knife

200ml [generous ¾ cup] full-bodied, fruity red wine

1.2 litres [5 cups] good-quality beef stock

1 bushy sprig of rosemary, needles picked and finely chopped

1 bay leaf

200g [1 cup] cooked beluga lentils (from a can or pouch, or cooked from dried)

100g [⅔ cup] dried cherries

60g [2 cups] shredded cavolo nero or kale

sea salt and freshly ground black pepper

Oak-Smoked Haddock

WITH LEEK & NEW POTATO

There's a predominance of fish in this book that betrays my seaside location. A walk along the Stade, where the day boats are winched straight out of the water and up onto the pebbly beach, reveals that many of the tall huts once used for drying nets have been converted into smokeries, their kinked silver flues snaking their way up the exterior walls. There exists here an endearing eagerness to smoke anything within arm's reach, but I'll happily eschew the array of smoked olives, cheese, hummus... for the fantastic fish. The hot-smoked salmon is probably the main event, but the oak-smoked haddock deserves honourable mention and is flavoursome enough that you don't need too much to add a deep smoky fishy flavour to this lighter version of a chowder.

Heat the oil and butter in a large saucepan set over low heat and sauté the onion, leeks and garlic gently for about 10 minutes or so until everything is well softened.

Add the milk, jelly stock, potatoes and bay leaves, put the lid on the pan and increase the heat to medium–high to bring the liquid to a simmer, but don't let it boil. Once simmering, turn down the heat and leave to simmer gently for 15 minutes or so, or until the potatoes are just a couple of minutes off being completely tender.

Add the peas and the fish and cook for about 4 minutes until the fish is just cooked. Remove it with a large slotted spoon or strainer and flake it into pieces. Add it back to the pan, along with the parsley and the lemon zest. Season the soup well with a little salt (if needed – the fish will be quite salty), plenty of black pepper, a little grated nutmeg and a squeeze of lemon juice.

Ladle the soup into warmed bowls to serve.

SERVES 4

1 Tbsp olive oil
1 Tbsp butter
1 large onion, diced
2 leeks, finely sliced
2 garlic cloves, finely chopped
1.2 litres [5 cups] whole milk
½ jelly vegetable stock pot
160g [5½oz] small new potatoes, sliced in half (I use the mini ones, but if yours are a bit bigger, just quarter them)
2 bay leaves
100g [¾ cup] frozen peas
300g [10½oz] oak-smoked haddock (in one large piece), skinned and boned
a large handful of flat-leaf parsley leaves, roughly chopped
zest of 1 lemon, plus a squeeze of the juice
grated nutmeg, to season
sea salt and freshly ground black pepper

Goat Mole Soup

WITH PINTO BEANS

There's a bit of a goat dilemma in the UK. While goat's cheese is universally loved, not much of a market exists for the meat, meaning something deeply regrettable has to happen to the little billy goats who lack the requisite apparatus for milk production. As I'll happily sit down to a goat's cheese pizza, I try and eat a bit of goat meat occasionally to attempt to mitigate some of the devastating food waste that's become an unfortunate by-product. This is all very unjust, I might add, as it's a delicious and underrated meat, and especially suited for cooking long and slow like this. My local butcher sells 1kg [2¼lb] bags of mixed goat meat and bones, which make a great base for this soup with a Mexican chocolate–chilli twist.

Heat 1 Tbsp of the oil in a large saucepan and brown half of the goat meat and bones for a few minutes, until they have picked up some colour. Remove from the pan with tongs, add another 1 Tbsp of oil, if you need to, and brown the second half.

Return all the goat to the pan and cover with 1.5 litres [6½ cups] cold water. Add the halved onion, celery, carrot and bouquet garni. Put a lid on the pan and bring the water to the boil, then lower the heat so it is gently simmering and cook for 2 hours until the goat is really tender. Strain, reserving the stock, and shred the goat meat from the bones. Leave the stock to cool here if you can as it makes it much easier to remove any fat from the top. If you are cooking the soup straight away, use a spoon to skim off as much fat from the top as you can.

Put the stock into a clean pan and cook to reduce down until you have about 1 litre [4¼ cups].

Meanwhile, heat the remaining 1 Tbsp oil in the cleaned large saucepan and sauté the diced onion and garlic for about 10 mins until soft and translucent. Add the chilli paste, cumin, cinnamon and oregano and cook for another couple of minutes until it's smelling aromatic. Tip in the chopped tomatoes and stir in the cocoa powder.

Add the reduced stock to the pan and cook for 15 minutes, so the tomatoes have a chance to cook a bit more, then stir in the goat meat, pinto beans and almond butter. Taste and season well with salt and black pepper, then ladle into 4 warmed bowls. Serve topped with a few coriander leaves.

SERVES 4 | DAIRY-FREE

2–3 Tbsp olive oil
1kg [2¼lb] mixed goat meat and bones
2 onions: 1 halved, 1 diced
1 celery stick, chopped into chunks
1 carrot, chopped into chunks
a bouquet garni made from a bay leaf, thyme sprigs and parsley stalks
3 garlic cloves, finely chopped
1½ Tbsp ancho chilli paste
½ tsp ground cumin
½ tsp ground cinnamon
2 tsp dried Mexican oregano (or use standard)
1 x 400g [14oz] can chopped tomatoes
1½ Tbsp cocoa powder
1 x 400g [14oz] can pinto beans, drained and rinsed
2 Tbsp smooth almond butter
sea salt and freshly ground black pepper
coriander [cilantro] leaves, to serve

Creamy & COMFORTING

Red Hot Three Pepper Soup

WITH CHEESY POLENTA CROUTONS

The various peppers here add three different dimensions to what's actually a pretty simple soup: sweetness from the red [bell] peppers; smokiness from the pimentón; and heat from the chillies. You'd be forgiven, scanning a few of the recipe titles in this book, for assuming that I'm a bit of a chilli fiend. Truth be told, until relatively recently I was the one ordering the korma. So, I do empathize and heartily advise adding the chillies by degrees. Roast them all together but blend them in one at a time, tasting in between, and if the last one doesn't quite make it to the liquidizer, who's watching anyway?

Preheat the oven to 180°C fan (350°F) Gas 4.

Put the peppers and whole chillies on a baking sheet and drizzle with 1 Tbsp of the olive oil. Toss them around to make sure everything is well coated, then pop in the oven for 25–30 minutes, or until well softened and the skins are just beginning to char.

Meanwhile, heat the remaining olive oil in a large saucepan set over low–medium heat and add the onion. Cook for about 5 minutes until beginning to soften. Add the carrot, garlic and paprika, and continue to cook for about 5 minutes more. Raise the heat, add the stock, pop a lid on the pan and bring it to the boil, then lower the heat so that the liquid is simmering and cook for 10–15 minutes until the carrot is totally tender.

When the peppers are cooked, add them to the pan. If you are confident the chillies won't be too much, add them here too (whole is fine if you want the heat from the seeds, but do remove the stalks). If you'd like to add them a bit at a time, leave them out for now – they are already cooked so can just be blended in at the end.

Remove the pan from the heat and blend with a stick blender or transfer to a liquidizer and blitz until smooth. (Add the chillies here if you need to.) Taste and season with salt and black pepper.

Ladle the soup into warmed bowls and top with a few freshly cooked and still hot cheesy croutons. Serve the rest in a bowl on the side.

SERVES 4 | VEGETARIAN

5 red [bell] peppers, halved and deseeded
2–3 red chillies
3 Tbsp olive oil
1 onion, diced
1 large carrot, peeled and diced
1 garlic clove, crushed
1 Tbsp sweet smoked paprika (pimentón dulce)
800ml [3⅓ cups] vegetable stock
sea salt and freshly ground black pepper
1 quantity Cheesy Polenta Croutons (see page 12), to serve (optional)

Garlicky Cauliflower
WITH SALSA VERDE

This may sound like a peculiar combination, but I'd like to make its case anyhow. Cauliflower needs punchy flavours to lift it, and the slightly sour crème fraîche, salty anchovies and fresh herbs cut through any brassica sulphuriness that might be lingering stubbornly.

Heat the oil in a large saucepan set over low–medium heat and add the onion. Sauté for about 8 minutes until softened and translucent. Add the garlic and cauliflower, turn up the heat to medium–high and cook for a further 5 minutes or so until the cauliflower is well coated in the garlicky oil and is beginning to soften. Add the stock and bring to the boil, then lower the heat and simmer, covered, for about 12–15 minutes until the cauliflower is tender.

Meanwhile, make the salsa verde by combining the ingredients in a small bowl, adding as much red chilli as you like, if using. Season to taste – remembering that the anchovies are salty so you may not need too much salt – and set aside.

Once the cauliflower is tender, remove the pan from the heat and blend with a stick blender or transfer to a liquidizer and blitz until smooth. Stir in the crème fraîche, then season well with salt and pepper.

Serve the soup in warmed bowls with a good dollop of the salsa verde in the middle.

SERVES 4

2 Tbsp olive oil
1 large onion, diced
3 large garlic cloves, finely chopped
1 large cauliflower, cut into florets
1 litre [4¼ cups] hot vegetable stock
100g [½ cup] half-fat crème fraîche
sea salt and freshly ground black pepper

For the salsa verde:
½ (25g/1oz) bag basil, finely chopped
½ (25g/1oz) bag flat-leaf parsley, finely chopped
½ (25g/1oz) bag mint, finely chopped
4 Tbsp extra virgin olive oil
2 Tbsp freshly squeezed lemon juice
8 anchovies, finely chopped
1 Tbsp drained capers, finely chopped
¼–½ red chilli, deseeded and finely diced (optional)

Quick Cannellini & Za'atar

WITH EVEN QUICKER CHILLI & LEMON OIL

While I'm reluctant to consign any of the soups in this book to the dull, workaday basics bin, there's no getting around the fact that supper can't get much simpler than this. It relies on storecupboard staples (I know what you're thinking, but za'atar should be in your storecupboard! It costs no more than any other jar of herb mix and is widely available in supermarkets), so even if there's not much in the fridge, you'll probably be able to whip it up anyway. And if apathy is at an all-time high, there are some pretty good lemon and/or chilli oils on the market.

Combine all the ingredients for the chilli & lemon oil in a small bowl and set aside to infuse while you make the soup.

Heat the oil in a large saucepan set over medium–low heat. Add the onion, celery and garlic and cook for about 10 minutes, stirring frequently, until everything has softened.

Add 1 Tbsp of the za'atar to the pan and cook for 1 minute, then add the vegetable stock and cannellini beans to the saucepan and turn the heat up to bring the liquid to the boil. Lower the heat and simmer for about 5 minutes, until the beans are heated through. Blend with a stick blender, or transfer to a liquidizer and blitz until smooth. Season to taste with salt, pepper and a good squeeze of lemon juice. Taste and if you think it needs more za'atar, go ahead and add the last ½ Tbsp.

Ladle the soup into warmed bowls and drizzle some of the oil over the top. Finish with a little sprinkling of za'atar and serve immediately – this one doesn't benefit from sitting around.

SERVES 4 | VEGETARIAN

2 Tbsp olive oil
1 large onion, finely diced
1 celery stick, finely sliced
2 garlic cloves, finely chopped
1–1½ Tbsp za'atar, plus extra
    to sprinkle
700ml [3 cups] vegetable
    stock
2 x 400g [14oz] cans cannellini
    beans, drained and rinsed
a good squeeze of lemon juice
sea salt and freshly ground
    black pepper

For the chilli & lemon oil:
1½ tsp crushed chilli flakes
    [red pepper flakes]
finely grated zest of 1 lemon
3 Tbsp extra virgin olive oil

Roasted Carrot

WITH HAZELNUT & STAR ANISE

This is exactly what I'd want after a nippy, autumnal walk – or during, armed with a trusty Thermos. It does seem like a lot of star anise, but the little stars are extracted before you blend, so just imbue the soup with a subtle spiciness rather than launch a full anise assault. If a good loaf of sourdough will fit into the backpack too, all the better.

Preheat the oven to 190°C fan (375°F) Gas 5. Put the carrots in a roasting pan and drizzle with the 2 Tbsp of hazelnut oil. Season with salt and pepper and stir so that the carrots are fully coated. Pop in the oven and roast for 30–40 minutes until the carrots are tender and browning, stirring halfway through.

Meanwhile, tip the hazelnuts onto a baking sheet and roast, on the shelf under the carrots, for 5 minutes, until golden and smelling toasty. Let cool, then roughly chop them and set aside.

While the carrots are cooking, start the soup. Heat the light oil in a large saucepan set over a low heat and sauté the onion for 8 minutes until starting to soften. Add the sweet potato and cook for another couple of minutes, then tip in the stock. Add the star anise and cover with a lid. Increase the heat to high until the liquid is boiling, then decrease it to medium and leave the soup to simmer, still covered, for about 15 minutes, or until the sweet potato and onion are completely tender. Remove the pan from the heat.

Fish out the star anise from the soup and discard (or keep to decorate the bowls). Add the roasted carrots to the pan, then blend with a stick blender or transfer to a liquidizer and blend until smooth (you may need to do this in batches). Return the soup to a clean saucepan and season well with salt and pepper.

Ladle the soup into warmed bowls and sprinkle the roasted hazelnuts over the top of each bowl. Finish with a good drizzle of hazelnut oil and a sprinkling of black pepper to serve. If you're feeling fancy, you could pop one of the star anise on the top of each bowl to decorate as they are very pretty, but do warn people to leave those in the bowl and not bite into them!

SERVES 4–6 | VEGETARIAN

4 large carrots (about 750g/
   1lb 10oz), peeled and
   chopped into chunky batons
2 Tbsp hazelnut oil, plus extra
   to drizzle
50g [2oz] blanched hazelnuts
2 Tbsp light-flavoured oil,
   such as sunflower or
   rapeseed [canola]
1 onion, diced
1 smallish sweet potato (about
   150g/5½oz), peeled and diced
1 litre [4¼ cups] vegetable stock
6 star anise
sea salt and freshly ground
   black pepper

Fennel, Almond & Vanilla

WITH TOASTED ALMOND SPRINKLE

It was fully my intention to use a ready-made almond milk for this recipe to keep things simple, until I looked at a carton or two and realized how alarmingly little actual almond they contain – many are less than 2.5 per cent nuts. Not being especially keen to promote any lunch that's packed with preservatives, gums, gelling agents, etc., I propose here making your own – it's far more nutritious and natural, and not that much more expensive than the fake stuff. It does admittedly require some forward thinking, but what you get is a much creamier milk and a subsequently far superior soup.

Set aside a small handful of the almonds for the topping (about 30g/1oz). Put the remaining almonds in a bowl and cover with 800ml [3⅓ cups] water. Cover the bowl with a plate and leave the nuts to soak in the fridge overnight or up to a couple of days.

Once they have soaked, tip the almonds into a powerful blender and blitz for a couple of minutes until you have a smooth thick mixture. Pass it through a sieve lined with a muslin cloth [cheesecloth] (use a splash more water to swill out the mixer jug and tip that in too). Leave the milk to drip through (in the fridge) for a good while, then squeeze out the grounds in the cloth. You should be able to get about 700ml [3 cups] creamy milk out.

Heat the oil in a large saucepan over low–medium heat and add the onion, fennel, garlic and a good pinch of salt. Stir to coat in the oil, cover and cook for 15 minutes or so, stirring frequently, until all the veg are well softened. Add the almond milk, vegetable stock and potato and stir everything together well. Cook for another 10 minutes until the potato is cooked.

Meanwhile, slice the reserved almonds once or twice lengthways, so you have quite chunky slices. Heat a frying pan over medium heat and dry fry the almonds for about 5 minutes, watching and stirring continuously, until they are golden and smelling toasty. Once they are, remove them from the hot pan straight away.

Add half of the vanilla bean paste to the soup, then blend with a stick blender, or transfer to a liquidizer and blitz until smooth. Taste and add more vanilla if you like, but don't go OTT – it's supposed to be an aromatic hint rather than make the soup taste like a weird dessert. Season to taste and serve sprinkled with the toasted almonds and a few chopped reserved fennel fronds.

SERVES 4 | VEGETARIAN

300g [2¼ cups] whole
    blanched almonds
1 Tbsp olive oil
1 onion, diced
2 large fennel bulbs, diced
    (reserve the fronds)
1 large garlic clove, finely
    chopped
250ml [1 cup] light vegetable
    stock (preferably
    homemade)
1 small potato (about 100g/
    3½oz), peeled and diced
¼–½ tsp vanilla bean paste
sea salt and freshly ground
    black pepper

Beetroot, Coconut & Dill

WITH TINY LITTLE SCALLOPS

I'm a real fan of adding flavour afterwards (but not as an after-thought) to what are, fundamentally, classic soups. The scallops are to this what the flaming orange zest is to a Cosmopolitan. Sure, you can enjoy it without, but there's a reason earthy beetroot and sweet scallops are so commonly paired, and these little Patagonian ones are just so conveniently crouton sized...

Heat the oil in a large saucepan over low heat, add the onion and celery and cook for about 10 minutes until both are tender. Add the beetroot and cook for 5 minutes more.

Add the vegetable stock and pop a lid on the pan. Raise the heat to medium and cook for about 30 minutes, with the lid on, until the beetroot is tender.

Pour in the coconut milk, then transfer the soup to a blender and add the dill and a good pinch of salt and pepper. Blend until smooth, then taste and add more seasoning if you feel it needs it – it will take quite a lot.

Heat a drizzle of oil in a non-stick frying pan set over high heat. Once very hot, add the scallops and flash fry for about 3 minutes maximum, turning halfway through, until they are golden and caramelized on the outside.

Pour the soup into warmed bowls and top each with a quarter of the scallops, a teaspoon of yogurt and a few dill sprigs to serve.

SERVES 4

2 Tbsp olive oil, plus a drizzle for the scallops

1 large sweet white onion, diced

2 sticks celery, sliced

500g [1lb 2oz] peeled and diced beetroot [beet]

600ml [2½ cups] vegetable stock

1 x 400ml [14fl oz] can coconut milk

a big bunch of dill, stalks discarded and fronds roughly chopped, plus a few sprigs to serve

sea salt and freshly ground black pepper

1 pack Patagonian scallops, to serve

4 teaspoons Greek yogurt, to serve

Chipotle Sweet Potato

WITH TORTILLA CROUTONS

Ever-expanding international supermarket ranges are proof of a positive sea change in attitudes toward food in recent years. Few ingredients now are deemed too niche to include, and while you'd once (not all that long ago) be struggling to find wonderful ingredients such as chipotle morita chillies, they can now be bought on impulse by the casual, intrigued aisle browser, rather than having to be specifically hunted down by the foodie know-it-all. If you want actual heat, go for two chillies; for a gentle tingle and a hint of that amazing smoky chipotle flavour, just add the one.

Preheat the oven to 180°C fan (350°F) Gas 4.

Heat the oil in a large saucepan set over low heat and cook the onion and garlic very gently with a good pinch of salt for about 8 minutes, until softening. Add the spices and chillies and stir in, then add the sweet potato and cook for a couple of minutes, stirring until well covered in the spiced oil.

Add the stock, put a lid on the pan and bring the liquid to a boil. Once boiling, reduce the heat slightly and leave to simmer, still covered, for 15 minutes, or until the sweet potato is tender.

Meanwhile, put the tortilla quarters on a large baking sheet. Combine the oil and smoked paprika in a small bowl and brush this over the tortillas. Turn them over and brush the other sides, too, then sprinkle them generously with sea salt flakes. Pop the sheet in the oven and bake for 5–6 minutes. Turn them over and bake for a further 5–6 minutes, or until they are turning crisp and golden, then remove them from the oven and allow to cool (they will crisp up a little more as they cool down).

Once the sweet potato is cooked, blend the soup with a stick blender or transfer to a liquidizer and blitz until smooth. Add the lime zest and juice, season to taste and blitz again to combine.

Ladle the soup into warmed bowls and top with the chopped avocado. Snap the baked tortillas into shard-like croutons and scatter a few of them over the top of the soup, serving any extra in a bowl on the side. Finally, sprinkle the bowls with a few coriander leaves, and serve.

SERVES 4–6 | VEGETARIAN

2 Tbsp olive or rapeseed [canola] oil
1 large onion, diced
2 large garlic cloves, finely chopped
½ tsp ground cumin
½ tsp ground cinnamon
1–2 chipotle morita chillies, roughly chopped
800g [1¾lb] sweet potatoes, peeled and diced
1.2 litres [5 cups] vegetable stock
grated zest of 1 lime, plus a good squeeze of the juice
sea salt and freshly ground black pepper
chopped avocado, to serve
coriander [cilantro] leaves, to serve

For the tortilla croutons:
2 tortillas, cut into quarters
1 Tbsp olive oil
1 tsp sweet smoked paprika (pimentón dulce)
a good sprinkling of sea salt flakes

Sunshine Basil

WITH LEMON & EGG

There are not many scents on this planet that provoke a favourable response as strong as that which basil seems to inspire – and this positive feeling can only be intensified by using the punchier Greek variety. This is a take on the classic creamy and tangy Greek soup avgolemono, only with the basil ante well and truly upped. It may seem odd to add egg to a soup, but you can see a sort of sorcery at play as you stir in the eggs and watch the soup transform from watery broth to thickened, enriched elixir. Make sure you use the very best chicken stock for this – it is the base for the flavour.

Heat the oil and butter in a large saucepan set over a low heat and let the butter melt. Add the shallots and the garlic and sauté very gently for about 10 minutes – don't let them colour. Add the rice and stir to coat in the oil, then add the stock and simmer for about 10 minutes, or until the rice is almost tender. Turn the heat off (so you don't forget about it and let it start boiling) while you do the next bit.

Whisk the eggs in a bowl until light, then add the lemon juice and whisk in. Scoop up a ladle of the hot soup from the pan and trickle it slowly into the egg mixture, whisking as you go. Tempering the eggs like this will stop them curdling when they are added to the pan. Once you've added about 3 ladlefuls in the same way, tip the egg mixture slowly into the soup pan, again, stirring all the time as you go. Turn the heat back on so it is very low and cook incredibly gently until the eggs begin to thicken the soup a little – do not let it boil or the eggs will scramble. Add the lemon zest and season with salt and pepper.

Just before serving, stir in most of the basil leaves. Ladle the soup into 4 warmed bowls and top each one with a sprinkle of the remaining basil and a good grinding of black pepper.

SERVES 4

1 Tbsp olive oil
20g [1½ Tbsp] butter
3 echalion shallots, finely sliced
1 small garlic clove, finely chopped
75g [½ cup] white long-grain rice
1 litre [4¼ cups] good-quality chicken stock (homemade if at all possible)
2 large eggs
3 Tbsp lemon juice
zest of ¼ lemon
a small handful of Greek basil leaves, or finely shredded normal basil leaves

Wild Garlic

WITH POACHED EGGS & PINE NUTS

If you're not entirely sure what wild garlic looks like when it's not picked and packaged in plastic, it's worth doing a quick reccy on the internet for a picture of it in a more natural state. It grows quite prolifically in roadside hedges (wash it well) in many parts of the UK, so rather than walking obliviously past it, you could be sitting on a bit of a flavour goldmine. The shock of a vivid orange-yolked egg perched on top of the vibrant green was too fun to resist, but it does make this rather rich, so portions are kept advisedly modest.

Heat the oil in a large saucepan set over low heat and sauté the onion for a good 8 minutes or so until really softening. Add the stock and the rice and cook for 15 minutes, or until the rice is almost cooked but still has a little bite.

Meanwhile, pop the pine nuts into a small frying pan and dry fry over a medium heat, stirring and watching all the time, for about 4–5 minutes until they are turning golden and smelling toasty. Tip onto a plate immediately so they don't keep cooking.

Fill a pan about 5cm [2in] deep with water, add the vinegar and bring to a gentle simmer over medium heat, ready for the eggs.

Add the frozen spinach to the stock and rice and cook for about 3 minutes, until it has defrosted and the liquid is back up to simmering point. Turn off the heat, add the wild garlic and let it wilt in the heat of the liquid. Transfer to a liquidizer, or blend with a stick blender until smooth. Taste and season well with salt and pepper.

Cook the eggs 2 at a time so you don't get into a big mess. Take the first two and crack them each into their own small bowl. Gently lower the bowls, one at a time, into the water and gently tip out the eggs. Allow to cook for about 3 minutes, until the whites are set but the yolks remain runny. Fish them out gently with a slotted spoon and drain on a plate lined with kitchen paper. Repeat to cook the next 2 eggs.

Ladle the soup into warmed bowls and top each one with a poached egg. Sprinkle over the toasted pine nuts to serve.

SERVES 4 | VEGETARIAN

1 Tbsp olive oil
1 small onion, finely sliced
700ml [3 cups] vegetable stock
40g [¼ cup] Arborio rice
30g [¼ cup] pine nuts
1 Tbsp white wine vinegar
250g [about a 10oz package] frozen spinach
150g [5½oz] wild garlic
4 very fresh golden-yolked eggs
sea salt and freshly ground black pepper

Nigerian Spicy Peanut
WITH PLANTAIN CROUTONS

I offer my apologies to anybody reading this who is of Nigerian ancestry as this is almost certainly a mangling of a fine culinary canon. But I stand by it (well, perhaps not my first attempt...). It's got quite a kick, but the peanuts shine through and – as sugar has a magical way of balancing heat – the starchy sweetness of the plantain croutons dampens the fire. Perhaps we can compromise on 'Nigerian inspired'?

Preheat the oven to 200°C fan (400°F) Gas 6.

Heat the oil in a large saucepan and cook the onion with a good pinch of salt for about 8 minutes, or until softened and translucent. Add the garlic and chillies and cook for a couple more minutes, then add the cumin and fry for another couple of minutes until it's all smelling aromatic. Add the stock and sweet potato to the soup, put a lid on the pan, and let it bubble away for about 15 minutes, or until the sweet potato is tender.

Meanwhile, put the chopped plantain onto a baking sheet, drizzle with a little oil and sprinkle generously with salt. Pop in the oven and roast for 15–20 minutes, until golden and crisp, stirring halfway through.

Once the sweet potato is cooked, transfer the soup to a blender and liquidize until smooth. Add the peanut butter and season with salt and cayenne pepper, then blitz briefly again. Taste the soup and adjust the seasoning if necessary.

Pour the soup from the blender jug directly into bowls and top with the plantain croutons. Sprinkle with dried hibiscus, if using, to serve.

SERVES 4 | VEGETARIAN

2 Tbsp groundnut oil, plus a drizzle for the croutons
1 large onion, diced
3 garlic cloves, finely chopped
2 Scotch bonnet chillies (or more or less, depending on how hot you want it), sliced
¼ tsp ground cumin
1 litre (4¼ cups) vegetable stock
450g (1lb) white sweet potato, peeled and diced
1 large plantain, peeled and diced
4 Tbsp 100% natural sugar-free peanut butter (I use Meridian)
sea salt and cayenne pepper
dried hibiscus, to sprinkle (optional)

Jerusalem Artichoke

WITH WINTER SAVORY & DUKKA

*If you can't find winter savory, Jerusalem artichokes love sage, too, but as savory
is said to mitigate some of the more anti-social side effects of artichokes, it's worth
hunting it down. Try the local garden centre and plant up what's left of it. Dukka,
a gutsy Middle Eastern spice and nut mix, makes a great sprinkle for the top of
the bowl. There will most likely (and probably intentionally) be too much: If so,
dip flatbreads into oil, then into dukka to enjoy it Lebanese style.*

Heat the oil and butter in a large saucepan set over low heat and
add the onion and garlic. Sauté for a good 8 minutes or so until
the onion is soft and translucent. Add the artichokes and potato
and stir so they are coated in the oil, then add the stock, bay
leaves and savory. Pop a lid on the pan and leave to simmer for
about 20 minutes, or until the artichokes and potato are tender.

Meanwhile, make the dukka. Heat a small frying pan over
medium heat, add the hazelnuts and dry fry for a few minutes,
shaking the pan regularly, until golden brown and smelling
toasty. Tip then onto a chopping board and roughly chop, then
put them into a small bowl.

Add the cumin and coriander seeds to the pan and toast for a
few minutes until smelling aromatic and the seeds are starting
to pop. Tip them into a pestle and mortar and grind to a coarse
mixture, then add them to the bowl with the hazelnuts.

Add the sesame seeds to the pan and toast those for 1 minute or
so, until darkening slightly and smelling toasty. Tip them into
the mortar too and grind them a little, but keep some whole.
Tip the seeds into the bowl, add the salt and a good grind of
black pepper, and mix everything together.

Once the vegetables are cooked, fish out the bay leaves and
discard them. Transfer the soup to a blender (or use a stick
blender) and blend until very smooth, adding a splash of water
if you think it's a bit thick. Quickly pulse in some salt and
pepper, then taste and adjust the seasoning if needs be.

Pour the soup straight into 4 warmed bowls and top with
a sprinkling of dukka to serve.

SERVES 4 | VEGETARIAN

1 Tbsp olive oil
30g [1oz] butter
1 onion, diced
1 large garlic clove, finely
    chopped
750g [1lb 10oz] Jerusalem
    artichokes, peeled and
    diced
1 potato (about 150g/5½ oz),
    peeled and diced
1 litre [4¼ cups] vegetable
    stock
2 fresh bay leaves
a handful of winter savory
    sprigs, leaves picked and
    chopped (about 2 Tbsp)
sea salt and freshly ground
    black pepper

For the dukka:
35g [1¼oz] blanched hazelnuts
1 tsp cumin seeds
2 tsp coriander seeds
1½ Tbsp sesame seeds
1½ tsp sea salt flakes

Parsnip, Pear & Cardamom

WITH PEAR CRISPS

There's a line to be walked here to keep this warmly spiced and deeply comforting soup from becoming oversweet. You'd expect the sweetness to come from the fruit, but deceptively it's the parsnip that needs to be reined in. Get firm pears and they will actually add a touch of sharpness and lightness and prevent this from becoming stodgy. The crisps are a bit of fun; if you don't have a mandoline, don't sweat it – just serve standard croutons.

Start by getting the pear crisps baking. Preheat the oven to 100°C fan (200°F) Gas ½ and lightly grease a large baking sheet.

Slice two of the pears (leaving the skin on) thinly on a mandoline – you're aiming for 2mm [⅛in] max thickness. Lay the slices out on the prepared baking sheet and bake for 30 minutes. Turn them over and bake for another 30 minutes until dried (they will crisp up a little more as they cool down).

Meanwhile, heat the oil in a large saucepan set over a low heat and sauté the onion and garlic gently for 10 minutes, until the onion is softened and translucent. Add the parsnips and cardamom and stir together, then add the stock and cook for about 15 minutes until the parsnips are softened.

Meanwhile, peel, core and dice the remaining 2 pears.

Once the soup has had 15 minutes, add the diced pears and cook for 5 minutes more until the pears are softened. Transfer to a liquidizer and blitz until smooth, then taste and season with salt and black pepper and a good squeeze of lemon juice.

Serve the soup in warmed bowls, topped with the pear crisps and another good grind of black pepper.

SERVES 4 | VEGETARIAN

4 pears (slightly under-ripe)
1 Tbsp olive oil, plus a little
   for greasing
1 onion, diced
1 garlic clove, finely chopped
500g [1lb 2oz] parsnips, peeled
   and diced
black seeds from 6–8
   cardamom pods, ground
   in a pestle and mortar
1 litre [4¼ cups] homemade
   vegetable stock (see page 11)
a good squeeze of lemon juice
sea salt and freshly ground
   black pepper

Watercress & Mint

WITH HOT-SMOKED TROUT & LEMONY SHARDS

This soup may be my one concession to nostalgia in this book. On sweaty summer days when we were young, my sister and I would be herded into the family Nissan-Cherry-cum-sauna and ferried to the local river. There was a 'troll bridge' and a conveniently located watercress farm where Mum could stock up while us and Dad paddled. Her bounty was generally turned into something akin to this, and so as happy memories tend to rose-tint all around them, I have always loved the peppery taste of watercress. Combined with freshwater trout and garden mint, there's something undeniably English about this, excusing the fact that lemon trees weren't such a common sight along the banks of the River Chess.

Preheat the oven to 190°C fan (375°F) Gas 5.

Heat the 2 Tbsp oil in a large saucepan set over low heat and sauté the onion, with a good pinch of salt, for about 5–6 minutes or until beginning to soften. Add the garlic and continue to cook gently for about 5 more minutes, until the onion is soft and translucent.

Add the stock and potato to the pan, cover with a lid and turn up the heat up to high until the liquid is boiling. Once boiling, reduce the heat to medium and leave to simmer, still covered, for about 15 minutes until the potato is cooked.

Meanwhile, to make the lemony shards, rip the bread into small pieces and put them in a bowl with the olive oil. Season well with the sea salt flakes and toss everything together so that the bread is well coated in the oil. Spread the shards out on a baking sheet and bake for 10–12 minutes, or until turning golden and crispy. Remove them from the oven and stir in the lemon zest. Leave to cool on the sheet.

Once the potato is cooked, uncover the soup pan and add the watercress and mint, letting them wilt in the hot liquid for a few seconds. Use a stick blender, or transfer the soup to a liquidizer and blend until very smooth. Tip the soup back into a clean pan and season really well with salt and pepper.

Divide the soup between bowls and top each with a dollop of crème fraîche (if using), a quarter of the flaked trout, and a scattering of lemony shards, to serve.

SERVES 4 | DAIRY-FREE

2 Tbsp olive oil
1 onion, diced
1 garlic clove, finely chopped
900ml (scant 4 cups)
    vegetable or chicken stock
1 small potato (about 175g/
    6oz), peeled and diced
300g [10½oz] watercress
60g [2oz] mint, leaves picked
sea salt and freshly ground
    black pepper
crème fraîche, to serve
    (optional)
200g [7oz] hot-smoked trout,
    flaked, to serve

For the lemony shards:
1 thick slice of sourdough
    bread (about 150g/5½oz)
1 Tbsp olive oil
 a good pinch of sea salt flakes
finely grated zest of 1 small
    lemon

Creamy Fish Soppa

(IN A PSEUDO-SWEDISH STYLE)

Stockholmers know their seafood: unsurprising when you tot up the miles of sprawling coastline the archipelago boasts. They also know their soup – again, hardly a shock that soup should form part of the survival strategy for enduring austere Scandic noir winters. This is my Frankensoup, pieced together from the memory of the fish soups I tried when I was out there. It may not be exact, but it's pretty tasty anyway, and if you can't find fresh herring (don't try it with marinated herring – it makes the soup unpleasantly vinegary), feel free to use mackerel instead.

Heat a large saucepan over low heat and add the butter and oil. Once the butter has melted, add the onion, leek, fennel seeds and garlic and sauté gently for 10 minutes until everything is well softened.

Meanwhile, put the saffron in a small bowl with a splash of warm water and set aside to soak.

Add the white wine to the saucepan and turn up the heat to medium–high. Continue to cook for a few minutes until almost all the liquid has evaporated. Pour in the fish stock and stir in the tomato purée and potato cubes. Bring the liquid to the boil, then lower the heat to a gentle simmer and leave to bubble away for about 20 minutes, or until the potato is tender.

Once the potato is cooked, and with the heat still quite low, add the soured cream, stirring in well until it is fully incorporated. Add the saffron and its soaking water, along with the salmon, herring and mussels, pop the lid back on the pan and cook for about 4 minutes, until all the fish is just cooked through and the mussels have opened. Stir in the dill and season to taste with salt and pepper.

Ladle the soup into 4 warmed bowls (discarding any mussels that haven't opened as you go) and top each bowl with a dollop of aïoli. Serve with plenty of buttered rye bread on the side.

SERVES 4

30g [2 Tbsp] butter
1 Tbsp olive oil
1 onion, diced
1 leek, finely sliced
½ tsp fennel seeds
2 garlic cloves, finely chopped
a good pinch of saffron
150ml [⅔ cup] white wine
1 litre [4¼ cups] good fish
    stock
2 Tbsp tomato purée [paste]
1 floury potato (about
    200g/7oz), peeled and diced
    into 1.5cm [⅝in] cubes
100ml [scant ½ cup] soured
    cream
200g [7oz] boneless salmon,
    cut into chunks
200g [7oz] boneless herring
    fillets, cut into chunks
450g [1lb] mussels in their
    shells
a large bunch of dill, chopped
sea salt and freshly ground
    black pepper
aïoli, to serve
well-buttered rye bread,
    to serve

lovage leaves & seeds

WITH CRUNCHY ROASTED CHICKPEAS

When I first conceived this soup, I was under the misbelief that lovage leaves and ajwain seeds (often called lovage seeds) were from the same plant. As it turns out, they're not. But by this point I had already tested and found them to be a lovely combination, so any dearth of botanical expertise now seems irrelevant. Lovage has a strong celery-like flavour, which sits surprisingly well with the aromatic, herby flavour of ajwain. They both pack a powerful flavour punch, so the simple roasted and salted chickpeas provide a blandly calming influence.

To roast the chickpeas, preheat the oven to 190°C fan (375°F) Gas 5.

Put the chickpeas on a baking sheet and drizzle with olive oil. Pop the sheet in the hot oven and roast for about 20 minutes, shaking the sheet a couple of times during cooking, until they are turning crisp and golden.

Meanwhile, heat the oil for the soup in a large saucepan over low heat and add the onion, garlic and ajwain seeds. Cook gently for 10 minutes, until the onion is softened and translucent.

Add the stock and rice to the pan and cook for about 15 minutes, or until the rice is almost cooked. Add the peas and lovage and bring the liquid back up to the boil, then cook for 2 minutes, until the lovage is wilted and the peas are tender.

Transfer the liquid to a blender, add the lemon zest and blitz until smooth. If the soup's too thick, add a splash of hot water to loosen a little. Taste and season with salt and pepper and a squeeze of lemon juice.

Once the chickpeas are cooked, remove them from the oven and sprinkle with sea salt flakes.

Pour the soup into warmed bowls and sprinkle each bowl with a few chickpeas, serving any extra on the side.

SERVES 4 | VEGETARIAN

2 Tbsp olive oil
1 onion, diced
2 garlic cloves, finely chopped
1½ tsp ajwain seeds
800ml [3⅓ cups] hot vegetable
    stock
50g [2oz] Arborio rice
250g [9oz] garden peas
50g [2oz] lovage leaves
½ tsp lemon zest, plus a
    squeeze of juice
sea salt and freshly ground
    black pepper

For the roasted chickpeas:
1 x 400g [14oz] can chickpeas
    [garbanzo beans], drained
    and rinsed
a drizzle of olive oil
sea salt flakes

Simple Creamed Corn

WITH CUMIN

Cornbread fresh from the oven; blackened cobs straight off the barbecue; popcorn on a family film night... Then there's the wonderfully gloopy Chinese-style chicken and sweetcorn soup from the local takeaway that magically appeared on days off sick. I was trying to work out why the most absurdly simple soup in the book is one of the most satisfying and the answer, of course, is its primary ingredient – a taste that's so bound up in childhood memory, its sweetness making it one of the few vegetables kids will eat (almost) without question. While the chef in me is itching to add a few more ingredients to this soup, there's no added frills that I can think will actually improve it.

Heat the oil in a large saucepan over a low heat and add the onion. Sauté for about 5 minutes until beginning to soften. Add the garlic and cumin and cook for another 5 minutes or so until the onion is fully tender.

Add the stock and turn the heat up to high to bring the stock up to the boil. Once boiling, add the sweetcorn and reduce the heat slightly so it is simmering. Leave to bubble away for about 15 minutes, or until the sweetcorn is very tender.

Remove the pan from the heat and blend with a stick blender, leaving a bit of texture, like creamed corn, rather than a completely smooth liquid. You could do this in a blender or food processor too, but use a restrained pulsing rather than a full-on blitz.

Taste and season well with salt and pepper, then ladle into warm bowls and serve exactly as it is.

SERVES 4 | VEGETARIAN

2 Tbsp olive oil
1 onion, roughly diced
1 large garlic clove, finely diced
2 tsp ground cumin
1 litre [4¼ cups] vegetable stock
500g [1lb 2oz] frozen 'supersweet' sweetcorn
sea salt and freshly ground black pepper

Spiced Roasted Pumpkin
WITH GOAT'S CHEESE & MAPLE SEED BRITTLE

This is thick, sweet, fragrant and totally nourishing. The tangy goat's cheese and a hit of parsley help to add sharpness and freshness and lift it, but on the darkest days, you'd be forgiven for replacing such trimmings with a chunk of warm, crusty bread.

Make the brittle first as it needs time to cool. Preheat the oven to 160°C fan (325°F) Gas 2–3 and grease a non-stick baking sheet with a little oil.

Put the pumpkin seeds in a bowl with the maple syrup and add a pinch of cayenne pepper. Mix everything together, then pour onto the prepared baking sheet. Pop in the oven for 10 minutes.

Meanwhile, put the diced pumpkin on a large baking sheet and drizzle over 2 Tbsp of the olive oil. Sprinkle over the cumin, cinnamon and paprika and add a good pinch of salt and pepper. Stir it all together so the pumpkin is well coated in the spices.

Once the seeds have had their 10 minutes and are turning golden and the syrup is hot and bubbling, remove them from the oven and immediately tip them onto a piece of non-stick baking parchment. Sprinkle with sea salt flakes and leave to cool and set. Turn the oven up to 180°C fan (350°F) Gas 4 and put the pumpkin in the oven. Roast for about 35–40 minutes, or until tender, stirring halfway through cooking.

Towards the end of the pumpkin cooking time, heat the last 1 Tbsp olive oil in a large saucepan set over low heat. Add the onion and garlic and sauté gently for about 8 minutes until the onion is well softened. Add 800ml (3⅓ cups) of the stock and bring the liquid up to the boil, then add the cooked pumpkin. Leave to simmer for 5 minutes or so, to be sure the onion is tender throughout, then transfer everything to a liquidizer and blitz until smooth. Add a little more stock and blend again if you feel the soup is a bit thick. Return to the cleaned pan and season with a good squeeze of lemon juice and salt and pepper to taste, and reheat if necessary before serving.

Ladle the soup into bowls and crumble over a little goat's cheese, followed by a little of the maple brittle. Finish with a good grind of black pepper and a sprinkle of parsley to serve.

SERVES 4 | VEGETARIAN

700g [1½lb] peeled and diced
   pumpkin or butternut
   squash
3 Tbsp olive oil
1 tsp ground cumin
1 tsp ground cinnamon
1 tsp sweet smoked paprika
   (pimentón dulce)
1 onion, diced
2 garlic cloves, finely chopped
800–900ml [3–4 cups]
   vegetable stock
a squeeze of lemon juice
sea salt and freshly ground
   black pepper
80g [3oz] soft goat's cheese,
   to serve (opt for a
   vegetarian alternative
   if necessary)
chopped flat-leaf parsley,
   to serve

For the maple seed brittle:
a little oil, for greasing
40g [¼ cup] pumpkin seeds
2 tsp maple syrup
a pinch of cayenne pepper
a pinch of sea salt flakes

Malay Squash Chowder
WITH COCONUT & LEMON GRASS

Perhaps 'chowder' is a stretch here, but there aren't many other nouns that immediately conjure that sense of warmth and richness that a singular bowl of this soup can bring. I have left out the shrimp paste (used heavily in traditional Malaysian cooking) to keep it vegan, but you can add it in, if you like. In lieu of it, tamarind and miso pastes help to deepen the flavour.

Start by making the spice paste. Blend all the ingredients together in a mini chopper or small bowl of a food processor until you have a smooth paste.

Tip the paste into a large saucepan and cook over low heat for about 3 minutes, until it starts to smell lovely and aromatic. Add the stock, coconut milk and cream, tamarind paste and butternut cubes and increase the heat to medium. Pop a lid on the pan and bring the liquid to the boil, then lower the heat so that the mixture is simmering and leave it to bubble away for a good 30–35 minutes until the butternut is really soft and tender.

Mix the cornflour with a small splash of water and stir until dissolved, then add this to the soup along with the gula melaka and miso paste. Stir in and continue to cook gently for a couple more minutes until the soup has thickened slightly, then season to taste with salt.

Ladle the soup into warmed bowls and serve topped with fresh coriander leaves.

SERVES 4–6 | VEGETARIAN

500ml [2 cups] vegetable stock
1 x 400g [14oz] can coconut milk, plus 4 Tbsp thick coconut cream from the top of another can
2 tsp tamarind paste
600g [21oz] peeled and diced butternut squash
1 Tbsp cornflour [cornstarch]
½ Tbsp gula melaka (coconut palm sugar) or dark muscovado sugar
1 Tbsp white miso paste
sea salt
coriander [cilantro] leaves, to serve

For the spice paste:
2 Tbsp vegetable oil
3cm [1¼in] piece of fresh galangal, peeled and roughly chopped
2 lemon grass stalks, roughly sliced
2cm [¾in] piece of fresh turmeric, peeled and roughly chopped
2 garlic cloves, roughly chopped
2cm [¾in] piece of fresh ginger, peeled and roughly chopped
3 echalion shallots, peeled and roughly chopped
1–2 dried chillies, roughly chopped

Mushroom & Chestnut

WITH STILTON RAREBIT

The chestnut very much takes a supporting role in this soup, but its presence is undeniable, pepping things up with an underlying creamy, nutty richness while the earthy flavour of mushroom and piney scent of rosemary are allowed to sing.

Put the 20g [1½ Tbsp] butter and the oil in a large saucepan set over low heat and let the butter melt. Add the onion, garlic and rosemary and sauté gently for about 8 minutes until the onion is well softened. Add the mushrooms, turn up the heat a little and continue to cook for a further 5 minutes until the mushrooms are wilted and beginning to take on some colour.

Add the vegetable stock to the pan and bring to the boil, then lower the heat and simmer for a few minutes until everything is well cooked.

Meanwhile, toast the bread for the rarebits in a toaster or under a grill [broiler]. Put the butter in a bowl and beat in the mustard, then crumble in the cheese and mix until well combined. Add a tiny splash of milk, if that helps bring it all together into a spreadable mixture, then spread the cheese over the toast. Set aside until you are ready to serve.

Stir the chestnut purée into the soup, and transfer everything to a liquidizer. Blend until smooth, then taste and season well with salt and pepper.

Just before serving, toast the rarebits under a hot grill for about 2 minutes, or until the cheese is melted and bubbling and turning golden on top. Serve them with the soup for dipping.

SERVES 4 | VEGETARIAN

20g [1½ Tbsp] butter
1 Tbsp olive oil
1 large onion, diced
2 large garlic cloves, finely
  chopped
2 tsp finely chopped rosemary
5 large flat field mushrooms
  (about 400g/14oz) , chopped
800ml [3⅓ cups] vegetable
  stock
200g [7oz] cooked chestnut
  purée
sea salt and freshly ground
  black pepper

For the rarebits:
4 small or 2 large slices
  wholegrain sourdough
25g [2 Tbsp] butter, softened
½ tsp Dijon mustard
80g [3oz] Stilton cheese (opt
  for a vegetarian alternative
  if necessary)
a splash of milk, if needed

Confit Tomato
WITH THYME

This soup is an attempt to distil that heady scent of tomatoes at the height of the season when they are at their very best; to concentrate and sweeten that amazing flavour. And while it might seem counterproductive to spend two hours cooking the tomatoes to reduce the liquid and concentrate the flavour, only to then reconstitute it into a soup, this is depth of flavour you can't achieve by boiling up tomatoes and stock.

Preheat the oven to 120°C fan (250°F) Gas 1.

Spread the tomato halves over a large roasting pan, cut side up, and dot the onion halves and garlic cloves in the spaces between. Sprinkle over the thyme sprigs, then drizzle the oil over everything. Sprinkle over the sugar, if using, and a good pinch of salt. Pop in the oven and bake for about 2 hours, or until the tomatoes are well cooked, smell sweet and are beginning to collapse.

Extract the garlic cloves from the pan. Squeeze the garlic cloves out of their skins. Tip the tomatoes, thyme, garlic and any juices in the roasting pan into a liquidizer. Pour 300ml [1¼ cups] hot water into the roasting pan and use a spatula to scrape any juices and baked bits up off the bottom of the pan. Pour all this into the liquidizer, too. Blend until smooth, adding a splash more hot water if needed to get it to a nice smooth but thick consistency. Taste and season well with salt and pepper.

If necessary, tip the soup into a clean pan set over low heat and heat gently to rewarm, then serve.

SERVES 4 | VEGETARIAN

1.4kg [3lb 2oz] very ripe, very
    red vine tomatoes (about
    15 large ones), sliced in half
2 small red onions, halved
4 large garlic cloves, unpeeled
several bushy sprigs of soft
    summer thyme
4 Tbsp olive oil
a pinch of dark brown sugar
    (you may not need this if
    the tomatoes are very ripe
    and sweet)
sea salt and freshly ground
    black pepper

Index

PUBLISHING DIRECTOR Sarah Lavelle
COMMISSIONING EDITOR Céline Hughes
DESIGN & ART DIRECTION Emily Lapworth
PHOTOGRAPHER Luke Albert
PROP STYLIST Agathe Gits
FOOD STYLIST Rebecca Woods
PRODUCTION CONTROLLER Tom Moore
PRODUCTION DIRECTOR Vincent Smith

Published in 2018 by Quadrille,
an imprint of Hardie Grant Publishing

Quadrille
52–54 Southwark Street
London SE1 1UN
quadrille.com

All rights reserved. No part of this publication
may be reproduced, stored in a retrieval
system or transmitted in any form by any
means, electronic, mechanical, photocopying,
recording or otherwise, without the prior
written permission of the publishers and
copyright holders. The moral rights of
the author have been asserted.

Cataloguing in Publication Data: a catalogue
record for this book is available from the
British Library.

Text © Rebecca Woods 2018
Photography © Luke Albert 2018
Design © Quadrille 2018

ISBN 978-1-78713-268-9

Printed in China